Z-kai
Zoom-Up Workbook
Math

Grade
3

◼ Introduction

— Z-kai Values Thinking Skills and a Disposition for Learning —

Z-kai's **Zoom-Up Workbook** is tailored to develop students' mathematical thinking, problem solving, and explanation skills that are necessary for their future success in STEM. This series contains many problems that challenge students, because the problem solving requires them to apply mathematical concepts and develop skills that are uncommon to the mathematics curricula and instruction of most schools and classrooms. This series was developed to reflect or surpass grade-specific Common Core State Standards in Mathematics (CCSS-M, 2010). The application of mathematical reasoning, problem solving, and explaining mathematics provides multiple opportunities for students to apply the CCSS-M Standards for Mathematical Content and Practice.

Z-kai has provided educational services in Japan since its inception in 1931, particularly focused on developing challenging material for advanced and gifted PreK-12 students. Z-kai's extensive experience focuses on students' developing two important lifelong learning skills: (1) problem solving, reasoning, and flexible thinking; and (2) a disposition for curiosity, independent study and research, and collaboration with others to solve challenging problems. Through its success in educating more than 200,000 Japanese students each year, Z-kai has learned that it is better for students to solve a limited number of well-thought-out problems rather than numerous less-challenging ones. In this way, students' mathematical knowledge, thinking skills, and processing are maximized and made more flexible.

This Zoom-Up Workbook contains 45 challenging problem sets that have been carefully selected to optimize students' understanding and perseverance. Given a limited number of total problems, the focus is on depth of understanding rather than breadth of completion. Solving challenging tasks will help students develop confidence and motivation.

Another strength of Zoom-Up Workbooks is that many of the problems relate to the daily life of students. Applying previously-learned mathematics knowledge and skills to solve problems encountered in our daily lives helps students to see mathematics as useful and effective. Just as importantly, students develop interest and an eagerness for applying mathematics outside of the classroom, as well as in.

Solving challenging story problems develops students' mathematical practice that is necessary for success in middle school and beyond.

This workbook aims not only to build knowledge of algebra and geometry, but also to develop the following mathematical practice:

- Problem Solving Skills: Looking for necessary prior knowledge and utilizing this knowledge to solve new problem(s) that students have not yet learned to solve.
- Reading, Comprehension, and Representation Skills: Comprehending mathematics problem situations and representing them in diagrams, tables, graphs, and expressions.
- Explanation Skills: Explaining and justifying mathematical thinking processes and solutions.
- Comparison and Generalization Skills: Finding effective, better, and more efficient solution processes.

These skills are required in middle school and upper-level mathematics; therefore, it is important to refine and solidify these skills during the elementary school years.

How to use Z-kai Zoom-Up Workbook

1 This Zoom-Up Workbook contains 45 problem sets. We recommend that you solve problems starting with the first problem set (Problem 01) in the workbook. The problems are challenging, so please take your time and don't easily give up on finding the solutions. It might take you a few days to solve each problem set.

2 After you finish one problem set, check your answers by referring to the pages in the "Answers and Solutions" section at the back of the workbook.

3 If an answer is wrong, carefully read the section "How to Think and Solve" before reviewing your solution process. It is a good idea not to erase any mistakes in your work. Instead, use a different colored pen or pencil to make corrections and/or make notes to explain your mistakes and how you corrected your thinking. By doing this, you will more clearly understand and remember the mathematics needed to solve the problem(s).

4 In each section titled **If you can solve this, the math - *and you* - are cool!** or **It's awesome if you know!**, you will find useful information that will help you understand and increase your learning.

5 The problems marked with the thumbs-up symbol 👍 are very challenging problems. When you figure out how to solve these problems, you should be very proud of your achievement.

Dear Parents, Dear Teachers,

The Z-kai Zoom-Up Workbook is designed for students to be able to work independently. The workbook provides an "Answers and Solutions" section that gives detailed explanations about how to think about and understand solutions to challenging problems. To develop good habits for learning mathematics' problem solving, we recommend that students check and compare their answers and solution process to the material in "Answers and Solutions." We also encourage parents and teachers to read the explanations together with students, especially since reading and comprehending explanations is challenging for all students, at least some of the time.

Since everyone should learn to enjoy the challenge of thinking about and solving challenging problems … let's solve challenging problems together!

Eamal Milmali Iwanko

Z-kai Zoom-Up Workbook Math Grade 3

Check!

1 Calculation Puzzles .... 6 ✓

2 Large Numbers Greater Than 1,000 (Part 1) .... 8 ☐

3 Large Numbers Greater Than 1,000 (Part 2) .... 10 ☐

4 Cool Calculation Methods .... 12 ☐

5 Algorithm Calculations (Addition) .... 14 ☐

6 Algorithm Calculations (Subtraction) .... 16 ☐

7 Challenge Yourself to Do Mental Calculations .... 18 ☐

8 Multiplication (Part 1) .... 20 ☐

9 Multiplication (Part 2) .... 22 ☐

10 Multiplication (Part 3) .... 24 ☐

11 Multiplication (Part 4) .... 26 ☐

12 Multiplication (Part 5) .... 28 ☐

13 Multiplication (Part 6) .... 30 ☐

14 Multiplication – At the Supermarket (Part 1) .... 32 ☐

15 Multiplication – At the Supermarket (Part 2) .... 34 ☐

16 Multiplication – At the Supermarket (Part 3) .... 36 ☐

17 Multiplication – At the Supermarket (Part 4) .... 38 ☐

18 Multiplication – Star Gazing (Part 1) .... 40 ☐

19 Multiplication – Star Gazing (Part 2) .... 42 ☐

20 Multiplication – Let's Play Cards (Part 1) .... 44 ☐

21 Multiplication – Let's Play Cards (Part 2) .... 46 ☐

22 Division (Part 1) .... 48 ☐

23 Division (Part 2) .... 50 ☐

24 Math Problems with Counters (Part 1) .... 52 ☐

25 Math and Camping (Part 1) .... 54 ☐

26 Math and Camping (Part 2) .... 56 ☐

27 Math Problems with Counters (Part 2) .... 58 ☐

28 Let's Plant Trees and Flowers! (Part 1) .... 60 ☐

29 Let's Plant Trees and Flowers! (Part 2) .... 62 ☐

30 Fractions (Part 1) .... 64 ☐

31 Fractions (Part 2) .... 66 ☐

32 A Rabbit and a Turtle Race to Wonderland Park (Part 1) .... 68 ☐

33 A Rabbit and a Turtle Race to Wonderland Park (Part 2) .... 70 ☐

34 Time and Elapsed Time .... 72 ☐

35 School-Related Math Problems .... 74 ☐

36 Going to Zoom-Up Park .... 76 ☐

37 Let's Go to the Sweet Factory! .... 78 ☐

38 Liquid Volume – On the Farm (Part 1) .... 82 ☐

39 Liquid Volume – On the Farm (Part 2) .... 84 ☐

40 Becoming a Master of Balance Scales (Part 1) .... 88 ☐

41 Becoming a Master of Balance Scales (Part 2) .... 90 ☐

42 Triangles and Quadrilaterals (Part 1) .... 92 ☐

43 Triangles and Quadrilaterals (Part 2) .... 94 ☐

44 Areas (Part 1) .... 96 ☐

45 Areas (Part 2) .... 98 ☐

Answers and Solutions 103

1 Calculation Puzzles

1 The sum of the 3 numbers on each ring are the same.
Fill in the blank ◯ with the appropriate numbers. (10 points for each ◯)

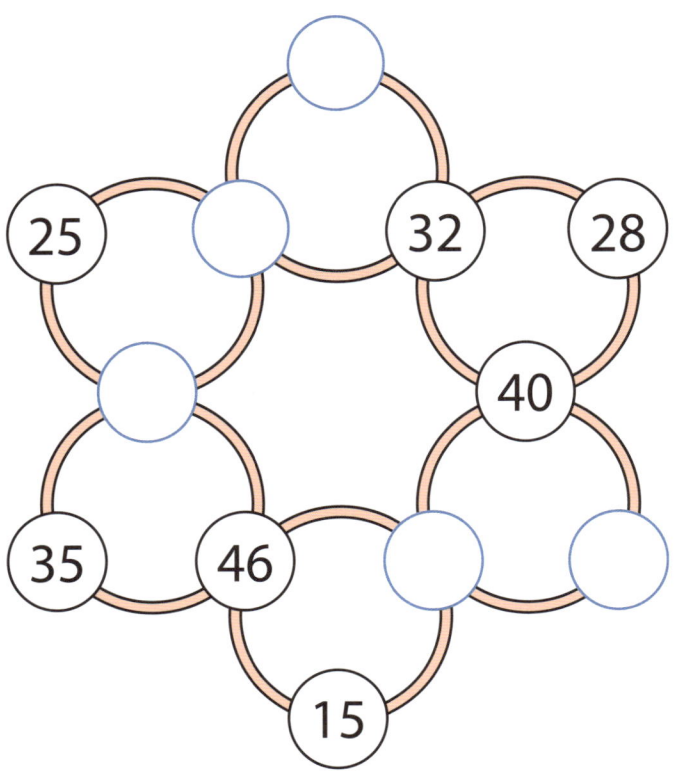

If you can solve this, the math - *and you* - are cool!

Look at the puzzle carefully and think about where to begin calculating. You may be surprised to see what a difference this makes.

2 The puzzle below will include all the numbers from 5 through 13 when it is completed. Fill in the blank boxes so the sum of the numbers in each row, column, and diagonal are equal. Some numbers from 5 through 13 are already placed in the puzzle. Fill in the blank boxes with the missing numbers to complete it. (25 points)

	11	
13	9	5
8		

3 Fill in the blank boxes with the numbers 1 through 16 to complete this larger puzzle. The sum of the numbers in each row, column, and diagonal need to be equal. Some of the numbers from 1 through 16 are already placed in the puzzle. (25 points)

	7	12	
11	2		8
	16		
4	9		15

What is the sum of the 3 numbers for problem **2** ?
What is the sum of the 4 numbers for problem **3** ?
This puzzle is called a "Magic Square."

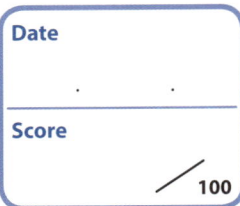

1 Put appropriate numbers in the ☐ below. (5 points for each ☐)

Ⓐ The number composed of 7 thousands and 2 ones is ⬚ .

Ⓑ The number that has 5s in the thousands and tens places and 0s in the hundreds and ones places is ⬚ .

Ⓒ The number 8,000 is made up of ⬚ hundreds.

2 Write the following number in standard form. (5 points for each ☐)

Ⓐ Nine thousand, six hundred, twenty-eight ⬚

Ⓑ Four thousand, seventy ⬚

3 Make 4-digit numbers using these four cards  .
What is the smallest 4-digit number you can make? (10 points)

You are not allowed to use the 0 (zero) digit in the highest place value.

Answer ⬚

4 Use the number line to answer the problems below.

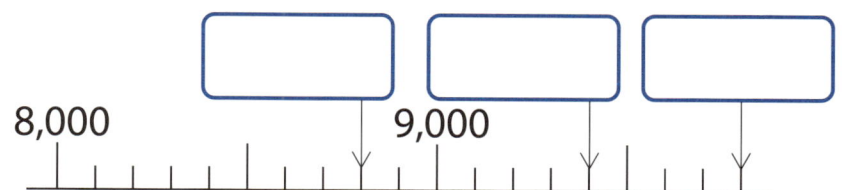

8,000   9,000

Ⓐ To complete the number line, put appropriate numbers in the ☐.
(5 points for each ☐)

Ⓑ Draw an arrow (↑) that points to 9,200. (5 points)

Ⓒ What number is 100 less than 9,200? (10 points)

Answer

Ⓓ How much greater is 9,200 than 8,800? (10 points)

Answer

5 Analyze the order of the numbers below and put appropriate numbers in the ☐.
(5 points for each ☐)

Ⓐ 9,000   8,000   [   ]   6,000   5,000

Ⓑ 9,600   [   ]   9,800   9,900   [   ]

Ⓒ 5,990   5,992   5,994   [   ]   5,998

Ⓓ 2,990   [   ]   2,980   2,975   2,970

3 Large Numbers Greater Than 1,000 (Part 2)

Date . .

Score /100

1 Put the appropriate inequality symbol (>, <) in the ☐ below. (5 points for each ☐)

Ⓐ 7,920 ☐ 8,000

Ⓑ 3,610 ☐ 3,520

Ⓒ 4,510 ☐ 4,501

2 Calculate the following. (5 points for each ☐)

Ⓐ 5,000 + 630 = ☐

Ⓑ 8,270 – 270 = ☐

Ⓒ 9,000 + 1,000 = ☐

Ⓓ 3,010 – 3,000 = ☐

Ⓔ 800 + 600 = ☐

Ⓕ 1,600 – 700 = ☐

Ⓖ 1,500 + 800 = ☐

Ⓗ 5,500 – 2,500 = ☐

Ⓘ 4,700 + 300 = ☐

J $10,000 - 9,900 = $

3 Calculate the following problems using the vertical algorithm (5 points each)

A
```
    2 3 0 0
  +   4 6 0
```

B
```
    9 8 1 6
  +   1 4 3
```

C
```
    2 0 9
  + 5 3 7 4
```

D
```
    3 7 2 8
  + 1 0 5 2
```

4 Calculate the following problems. (5 points for each ☐)

A $1,300 - (1,500 - 1,200) = $

B $1,500 + 3,400 + 500 + 4,600 = $

C $600 \times 4 = $

For problem **4** **C**, think about how many 100s will be in the answer: 600 is composed of six 100s, and there are 4 groups of 600.

11

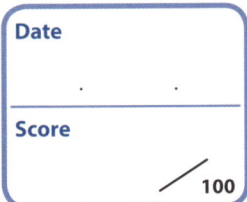

4 Cool Calculation Methods

1 At the end of the school year, a calculation competition will be held at Zoom-Up Elementary School. Bonita is good at mathematics and wants to become the champion. Bonita told her father about the competition at dinner. Her father taught her a cool calculation strategy.

A Read the dialogue the two are having. Put appropriate numbers in the ☐ below. (10 points each)

Father : You want to be a champion, don't you?

Bonita : Yeah! What can I do to prepare for the competition?

Father : If you know some smart calculation methods, I'm sure you will do well. Look at this addition problem. Can you solve it using mental math?

$$1 + 3 + 5 + 7 + 9 + 11 + 13 + 15 + 17 + 19$$

Bonita : This is an addition problem with 10 addends! If I can use mental math to solve a problem like this, I might be able to become a champion!

Father : I will give you a hint. Let's think about this problem!

When you add the first number and the last number, it is ①☐ .

When you add the second number from the front and the second number from the last number, it is ②☐ .

Do you notice anything?

Bonita : I see pairs of numbers that add up to the same sum. In this math sentence, there are ③☐ pairs that add up to ④☐ .

Father : Great! Can you find the answer to the problem?

B Use mental math to find the answer to the addition problem. (20 points)

$$1 + 3 + 5 + 7 + 9 + 11 + 13 + 15 + 17 + 19$$

(   )

C Bonita's father wants her to become a champion, so he gave Bonita the following challenging problem.

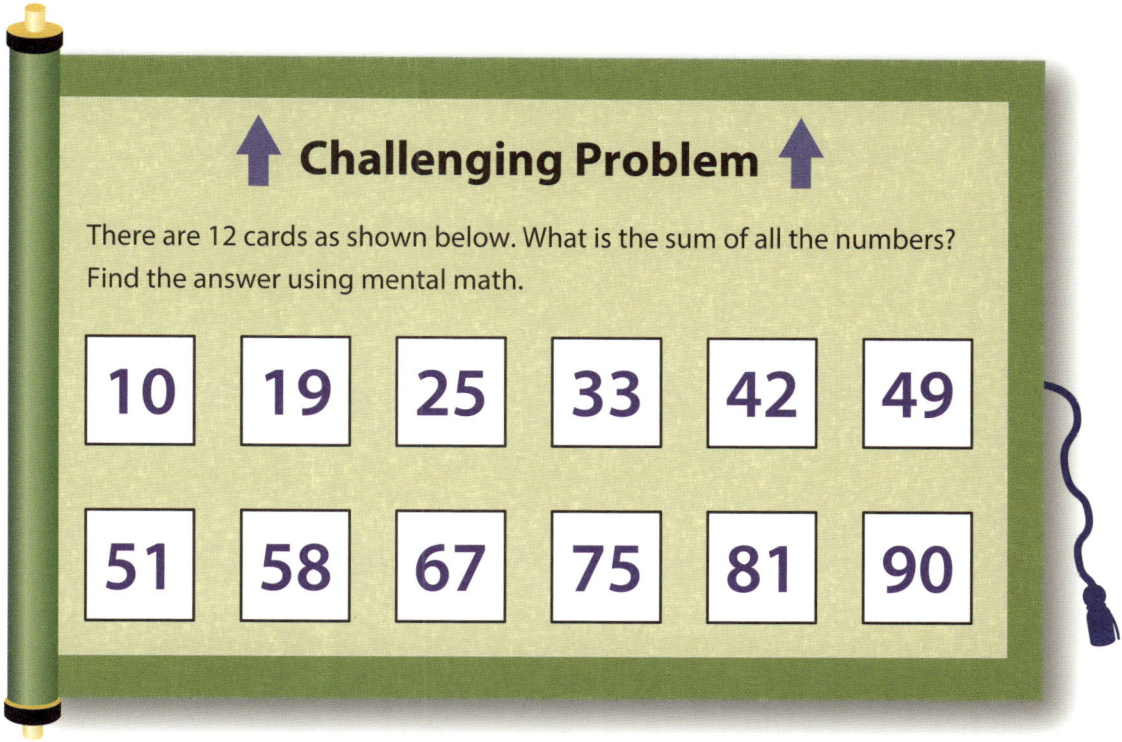

↑ **Challenging Problem** ↑

There are 12 cards as shown below. What is the sum of all the numbers? Find the answer using mental math.

| 10 | 19 | 25 | 33 | 42 | 49 |
| 51 | 58 | 67 | 75 | 81 | 90 |

Think about the Challenging Problem above.
Use mental calculation to find the answer. (40 points)

(   )

Algorithm Calculations (Addition)

Date

Score
/100

1 Calculate the following. (5 points each)

Ⓐ 194 + 738

Ⓑ 253 + 159

Ⓒ 388 + 73

Ⓓ 632 + 594

Ⓔ 506 + 845

Ⓕ 956 + 44

Ⓖ 1,256 + 5,376

Ⓗ 6,393 + 1,507

Ⓘ 5,183 + 2,862

14

2 Calculate the following. (5 points each)

A
```
   3 7 8 5
 + 4 5 6 3
```

B
```
   9 9 6 4
 + 2 6 5 8
```

C
```
   5 7 8 5
 + 4 2 1 5
```

3 Put appropriate numbers in the ☐ below. (10 points each)

A
```
   2 8 ☐
 + 3 4 5
   6 3 4
```

B
```
   ☐ 9 5
 + 7 ☐ 8
 1 2 2 3
```

C
```
   1 ☐ 2 4
 + 2 4 5 ☐
   4 2 8 0
```

D
```
   3 8 2 5
 + 4 ☐ ☐ 7
   8 4 1 2
```

15

6 Algorithm Calculations (Subtraction)

Date . .

Score / 100

1 Calculate the following. (5 points each)

Ⓐ 756 – 416

Ⓑ 693 – 375

Ⓒ 538 – 262

Ⓓ 830 – 825

Ⓔ 723 – 257

Ⓕ 864 – 289

Ⓖ 7,125 – 1,383

Ⓗ 3,452 – 2,904

Ⓘ 8,203 – 7,595

2 Calculate the following. (5 points each)

A
```
   5 7 6 1
 - 3 9 7 4
```

B
```
   9 7 3 4
 - 3 8 5 8
```

C
```
   4 0 0 0
 -   6 8 5
```

3 Put appropriate numbers in the ☐ below. (10 points each)

A
```
   8 9 ☐
 - 3 2 5
   5 6 8
```

B
```
   4 7 5
 - 2 ☐ ☐
   1 8 6
```

C
```
   5 ☐ 2 8
 - 2 4 6 ☐
   3 1 6 5
```

D
```
   6 4 3 5
 - 4 ☐ ☐ 7
   1 7 6 8
```

17

1 Instead of using the standard vertical algorithm, think about a better way to calculate the subtraction problem 1007 − 8. Put appropriate numbers in the ☐ below. (5 points for each ☐)

Divide 8 into ☐ and 1

$1,007 - 7 = 1,000$

☐ $- 1 =$ ☐ $\longrightarrow$ $1,007 - 8 =$ ☐

$1,007 - 8$

7 1

2 Think about a better way to calculate the following problems. (10 points each)

Ⓐ $1,005 - 7$

Ⓑ $1,003 - 6$

Ⓒ $1,002 - 8$

3 Think about a better way to calculate 997 + 999. Put appropriate numbers in the ☐ below. (5 points for each ☐)

> Step ① : Add <u>3</u> to 997 to make 1,000. Then, add <u>1</u> to 999 to make 1,000.
>
> Step ② : Subtract <u>3</u> and <u>1</u> that were added in step ① from the sum, 1,000 + 1,000.

$$997 + 999 = 1,000 + 1,000 - \boxed{} - \boxed{}$$

$$= \boxed{} - 3 - 1$$

$$= \boxed{}$$

4 Think about a better way to calculate the following. (10 points each)

Ⓐ 996 + 998

Ⓑ 497 + 499

Ⓒ 299 + 698

⭐ **It's awesome if you know!**

A better way to calculate 9,998 + 9,999

Let's think about how to calculate 9,998 + 9,999 in a clever way!
First, add <u>2</u> to 9,998 to make 10,000. Then, add <u>1</u> to 9,999 to make 10,000.
Now you can subtract 2 and 1 from the sum of 10,000 + 10,000.

$$9,998 + 9,999 = 10,000 + 10,000 - 2 - 1 = 20,000 - 2 - 1 = 19,997$$

In this way, you can calculate large numbers easily!

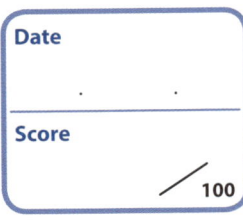

Date

Score

/100

1 Calculate the following. (3 points each)

Ⓐ 2 × 3

Ⓑ 5 × 8

Ⓒ 3 × 7

Ⓓ 6 × 6

Ⓔ 5 × 2

Ⓕ 8 × 4

Ⓖ 4 × 6

Ⓗ 2 × 9

Ⓘ 3 × 4

Ⓙ 5 × 5

Ⓚ 9 × 3

Ⓛ 8 × 2

Ⓜ 7 × 5

Ⓝ 6 × 4

Ⓞ 8 × 8

Ⓟ 9 × 7

Ⓠ 7 × 7

Ⓡ 4 × 9

Ⓢ 8 × 6

Ⓣ 9 × 9

If you can do these calculations quickly and accurately, you have perfectly mastered your multiplication facts!

2 The numbers in each problem follow a specific rule. Find each rule and put correct numbers in the ☐. (4 points each)

(A) 3   6   9   12   ☐   18   21   24   27

(B) 72   64   56   48   40   32   ☐   16   8

(C) 14   ☐   28   35   42   49

(D) 40   35   30   ☐   20   15

(E) 72   ☐   54   45   36

3 Think about the numbers in the multiplication facts of 3, 6, and 9.

(A) The products of the multiplication facts of 3 are shown below. Circle all products of the multiplication facts of 6. (10 points)

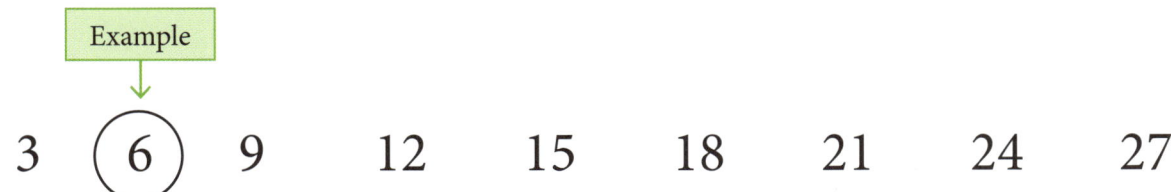

Example

3   (6)   9   12   15   18   21   24   27

(B) The products of the multiplication facts of 3 are shown below. Circle all products of the multiplication facts of 9. (10 points)

3   6   9   12   15   18   21   24   27

1 Put appropriate numbers in the ☐ below. (5 points each)

Ⓐ $5 \times \boxed{} = 20$

Ⓑ $2 \times \boxed{} = 18$

Ⓒ $3 \times \boxed{} = 21$

Ⓓ $7 \times \boxed{} = 42$

Ⓔ $6 \times \boxed{} = 42$

Ⓕ $\boxed{} \times 5 = 10$

Ⓖ $\boxed{} \times 8 = 32$

Ⓗ $\boxed{} \times 9 = 45$

Ⓘ $\boxed{} \times 4 = 28$

2 Put appropriate numbers in the ☐ below. (5 points for each math sentence)

Ⓐ Make math sentences that have a product of 24.

$\boxed{} \times \boxed{} = 24$

$\boxed{} \times \boxed{} = 24$

$\boxed{} \times \boxed{} = 24$

$\boxed{} \times \boxed{} = 24$

Ⓑ Make math sentences that have a product of 36.

$\boxed{} \times \boxed{} = 36$

$\boxed{} \times \boxed{} = 36$

$\boxed{} \times \boxed{} = 36$

3 You will multiply two numbers that are the same. Put appropriate numbers in the ☐ below. (5 points for each math sentence)

Example

$\boxed{2} \times \boxed{2} = 4$

Two identical numbers will be in these boxes.

Ⓐ $\boxed{} \times \boxed{} = 16$ Ⓑ $\boxed{} \times \boxed{} = 25$

Ⓒ $\boxed{} \times \boxed{} = 49$ Ⓓ $\boxed{} \times \boxed{} = 81$

It's awesome if you know!

Secrets of the multiplication facts of 3

Let's investigate products of the multiplication facts of 3 below.

3   6   9   12   15   18   21   24   27

For products greater than 10, the sum of the numbers in the tens and ones place equals a product in the multiplication facts of 3!

For example, let's choose the product 12: the sum of the tens and ones places will be $1 + 2 = 3$, which is a product of a multiplication fact of 3 ($1 \times 3 = 3$). Let's check other numbers in the same way:

15: $1 + 5 = 6$ (a product of the multiplication facts of 3)
18: $1 + 8 = 9$ (a product of the multiplication facts of 3)
21: $2 + 1 = 3$ (a product of the multiplication facts of 3)
Try checking other products such as 24 and 27!

$$12$$
$$\swarrow \searrow$$
$$1 + 2 = 3$$

A product of the multiplication facts of 3

Date

.   .

Score

/100

1 Put appropriate numbers in the ☐ below. (2 points for each ☐)

(A) $2 \times 6 = 12$ 12 is ☐ times as much as 2.

(B) $3 \times$ ☐ $= 12$ 12 is ☐ times as much as 3.

(C) $6 \times$ ☐ $= 12$ 12 is ☐ times as much as 6.

2 Put appropriate numbers in the ☐ below. (5 points for each ☐)

(A) The product of 2×5 is ☐ greater than the product of 2×4. If we express the relationship in a math sentence, it is written this way:

$2 \times 5 = (2 \times 4) +$ ☐

(B) $3 \times 7 = 3 \times 6 +$ ☐

(C) $4 \times 6 = 4 \times$ ☐ $+ 4$

(D) $8 \times 10 = 8 \times$ ☐ $+ 8$

(E) $8 \times 11 = 8 \times 10 +$ ☐

(F) $5 \times 7 = 5 \times 8 -$ ☐

(G) $6 \times 5 = 6 \times$ ☐ $- 6$

3 Put appropriate numbers in the ☐ below. (4 points for each ☐)

Ⓐ $(2 \times 2) \times 4 = 4 \times 4 = \boxed{}$

Ⓑ $2 \times (2 \times 4) = 2 \times \boxed{} = \boxed{}$

Ⓒ $6 \times 9 = (2 \times \boxed{}) \times 9$

Ⓓ $5 \times 9 = 5 \times (3 \times \boxed{})$

First calculate what is in the parentheses.

4 Think about how to calculate multiplication problems that have larger numbers. Put appropriate numbers in the ☐ below and calculate in a clever way. (5 points for each ☐)

Ⓐ $18 \times 4 = 9 \times \boxed{} \times 4 = 9 \times \boxed{}$

So, $18 \times 4 = \boxed{}$

Ⓑ $2 \times 21 = 2 \times \boxed{} \times 7 = \boxed{} \times 7$

So, $2 \times 21 = \boxed{}$

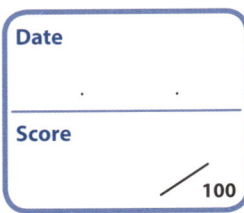

1 Pieces of a multiplication fact table are shown below.
Can you figure out what multiplication facts are represented by these pieces.
Find appropriate numbers for what is missing in the ☐ below. (15 points for each ☐)

A

| 20 | ☐ | 28 | ☐ |

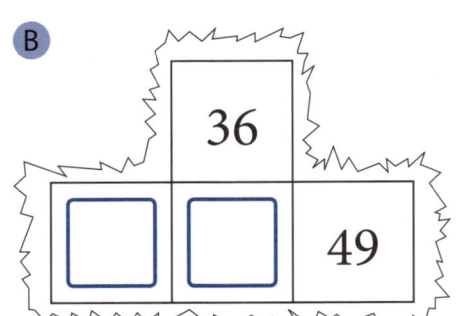

B

| 36 |
| ☐ | ☐ | 49 |

C

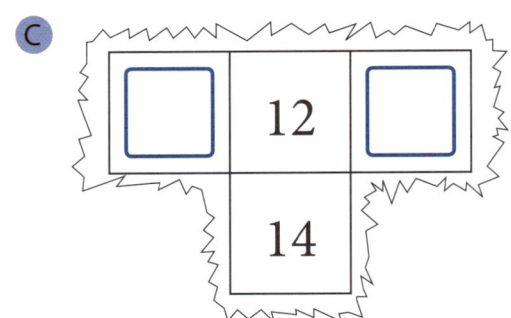

| ☐ | 12 | ☐ |
| | 14 |

The multiplication fact table starts with the multiplication facts of 1 in the top row, then goes on to 2, 3, 4, … 9.

⭐ It's awesome if you know!

Multiplying by 10

Multiplying numbers that are larger than the multiplication facts 1 – 9 can be done in a clever way. Let's calculate 3×10, 4×10 and 5×10.

$3 \times 10 = 3 \times 9 + 3 = 27 + 3 = 30$
$4 \times 10 = 4 \times 9 + 4 = 36 + 4 = 40$
$5 \times 10 = 5 \times 9 + 5 = 45 + 5 = 50$

$$\underline{3} \times \underline{10} = \underline{30}$$
multiplicand   multiplier   product

Study the wavy lines above. You will see how products of multiplying by 10 are the same as placing a zero (0) in the ones place of the multiplicand.
Can you explain why this happens?

2 Hana and Nathan are playing a multiplication card game. They are using a deck of cards that includes some 3-number multiplication problems and some two-digit numbers. Please read the rules below and figure out who is the winner. Write the winner's name in the ☐ below. (10 points)

How to play the game

1. Put multiplication cards face down.
2. Each player chooses one card.
3. The player with the greater product will get one point.
   If the products are the same, repeat steps 1 and 2.
4. Play 5 rounds. The player who has the greatest number of points wins.

	Hana's cards	Nathan's cards
1st	8 × 3	4 × 5
2nd	7 × 5	7 × 8
3rd	4 × 2 × 5	10 × 5
4th	9 × 9	2 × 27
5th	24 × 3	18 × 5

Hana   Nathan

Answer [ ]

Date

Score
/100

1 Study the diagram below. Complete each math sentence so it represents the diagram. Put appropriate numbers in the ☐ below. (5 points for each ☐)

A

There are 5 groups of 2.

 There are 5 groups of 1.

$3 \times 5 = (\boxed{} \times 5) + (\boxed{} \times 5)$

B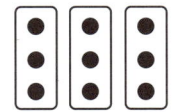

There are 3 groups of 3.   There are 2 groups of 3.

$3 \times 5 = (3 \times \boxed{}) + (3 \times \boxed{})$

2 Put appropriate numbers in the ☐ below. (5 points for each ☐)

A $4 \times 7 = (3 \times 7) + (\boxed{} \times 7)$

B $6 \times 5 = (6 \times \boxed{}) + (6 \times 3)$

C $3 \times 8 = (2 \times \boxed{}) + (1 \times \boxed{})$

D $\boxed{} \times 9 = (3 \times 9) + (4 \times 9)$

E $6 \times \boxed{} = (6 \times 4) + (6 \times 2)$

3 Put appropriate numbers in the ☐ below. (5 points for each ☐)

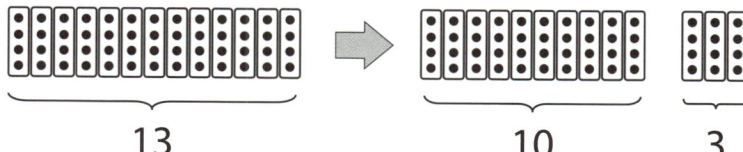

13   10   3

From the diagram above

$$4 \times 13 = (4 \times \boxed{}) + (4 \times \boxed{})$$

the answer for 4×13 is $\boxed{}$.

4 Put appropriate numbers in the ☐ below. (5 points for each ☐)

Ⓐ $6 \times 15 = (6 \times 10) + (6 \times \boxed{}) = \boxed{}$

Ⓑ $4 \times 12 = (4 \times \boxed{}) + (4 \times 2) = \boxed{}$

Ⓒ $18 \times 6 = (\boxed{} \times 6) + (\boxed{} \times 6) = \boxed{}$

> For problem Ⓒ, 18 can be split many different ways.
> I wonder how I can split the number to make the calcu-
> lation easier.

Date

Score

/100

1 Put appropriate numbers in the ☐ below. (3 points each)

(A) $3 \times \boxed{} = 18$

(B) $4 \times \boxed{} = 16$

(C) $9 \times \boxed{} = 54$

(D) $8 \times \boxed{} = 24$

(E) $7 \times \boxed{} = 63$

(F) $6 \times \boxed{} = 30$

(G) $\boxed{} \times 5 = 35$

(H) $\boxed{} \times 6 = 48$

(I) $\boxed{} \times 7 = 14$

(J) $\boxed{} \times 9 = 36$

(K) $\boxed{} \times 8 = 40$

(L) $\boxed{} \times 6 = 36$

2 Put appropriate numbers in the ☐ below. (4 points each)

(A) $6 \times 7 = 6 \times 6 + \boxed{}$

(B) $9 \times 3 = 9 \times 4 - \boxed{}$

(C) $7 \times \boxed{} = 7 \times 6 + 7$

(D) $4 \times 5 = \boxed{} \times 4$

(E) $\boxed{} \times 2 = 0$

(F) $5 \times \boxed{} = 0$

3 Calculate the following multiplication problems. (4 points each)

A 7×10

B 20×4

C 900×6

D 600×7

 **E** $4,000 \times 9$

 **F** $8,000 \times 6$

An easier and better way to calculate problems **C** and **D** is to think about how many groups of 100 there are. With problems **E** and **F**, think about how many groups of 1,000 there are.

4 Put appropriate numbers in the ☐ below. (4 points each)

A $2 \times 3 \times 4 = 2 \times 4 \times \boxed{}$

B $6 \times \boxed{} \times 8 = 6 \times 8 \times 7$

C $6 \times (\boxed{} + 4) = (6 \times 5) + (6 \times 4)$

D $\boxed{} \times 8 = (6 \times 8) + (3 \times 8)$

In problems **C** and **D**, calculate in the parentheses first.

Multiplication – At the Supermarket (Part 1)

1 Haley went to a supermarket near her house with her mom.
First, she went to the vegetable and fruit section.

A There are 4 apples in a basket. If Haley gets 3 baskets, how many apples will she get?
(10 points for the math sentence, 10 points for the answer)

Math Sentence

Answer ( )

B There are 3 cucumbers in a package. 5 people bought one package each.
How many cucumbers were sold altogether?
(10 points for the math sentence, 10 points for the answer)

Math Sentence

Answer ( )

C Haley buys 2 bunches of bananas. Each bunch has 5 bananas, how many bananas
does she buy altogether? (10 points for the math sentence, 10 points for the answer)

Math Sentence

Answer ( )

2 Next, she went to the fish section.

A There are 2 salmon fillets in a package. When there are 6 packages, how many salmon fillets are there altogether?
(10 points for the math sentence, 10 points for the answer)

Math Sentence

Answer ( )

B There is one lobster tail in a frozen package. When there are 7 packages, how many lobster tails are there altogether?
(10 points for the math sentence, 10 points for the answer)

Math Sentence

Answer ( )

33

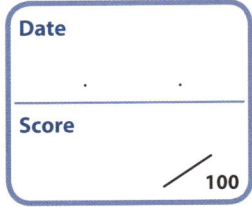

Date

.   .

Score

/ 100

1 Haley went to the frozen food section of her neighborhood supermarket.

Ⓐ She loves chicken nuggets! A box of frozen chicken nuggets includes 5 big nuggets. She buys 7 packages. How many chicken nuggets is that altogether?
(10 points for the math sentence, 10 points for the answer)

Math Sentence

Answer ( )

Ⓑ Frozen spring rolls come in a box. Each box contains 3 spring rolls. If Haley buys 4 boxes, how many boxes of spring rolls will she buy?
(10 points for the math sentence, 10 points for the answer)

Math Sentence

Answer ( )

Ⓒ Then she sees that a pack of frozen tacos contains 4 tacos! There are 6 packs on the shelf of the freezer. How many packs would she buy if she bought all of the packs?
(10 points for the math sentence, 10 points for the answer)

Math Sentence

Answer ( )

2 Haley found mochi ice cream in the freezer!

A Each small package of mochi ice cream contains only one piece of mochi ice cream. There are 9 packages in the freezer. How many packages of mochi ice cream are there altogether? (10 points for the math sentence, 10 points for the answer)

Math Sentence

Answer (   )

B In the freezer she also found larger packages of mochi ice cream. The larger packages contain 2 pieces of mochi ice cream. She sees 8 larger packages on the shelf. How many pieces of mochi ice cream are there altogether?
(10 points for the math sentence, 10 points for the answer)

Math Sentence

Answer (   )

I love mochi ice cream! I hope you get to try it too.
The answers to the multiplication facts of 1 are always the same as the multiplicands (the number being multiplied by 1). So, we don't really need to calculate to find the answer!

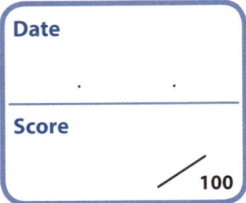

Date

Score

/100

1 Next, Haley went to the "Snack and Sweets" section!
She loves sweets and this is her favorite place in the market!

(A) She sees a box of chocolate chip cookies. It contains 9 cookies. If she buys 4 boxes, how many cookies does she get altogether?
(10 points for the math sentence, 10 points for the answer)

Math Sentence

Answer  (   )

(B) 8 pieces of rice crispie treats comes in one package. When there are 9 packages, how many treats are there altogether?
(10 points for the math sentence, 10 points for the answer)

Math Sentence

Answer  (   )

(C) Snack-sized cheese crackers come in boxes of 6 packs. If Haley buys 4 boxes, how many packs of snack-sized cheese crackers does she get?
(10 points for the math sentence, 10 points for the answer)

Math Sentence

Answer  (   )

D There are 9 pieces of chocolate in a box. When there are 7 boxes, how many pieces of chocolate are there altogether?

(10 points for the math sentence, 10 points for the answer)

Math Sentence

Answer

E A pack of gum contains 7 sticks of gum. When there are 3 packs, how many sticks of gum are there altogether? (10 points for the math sentence, 10 points for the answer)

Math Sentence

Answer

1 Haley's friend, Noah, loves to think of multiplication problems when he goes to the supermarket, too! First, he went to the bread section and then the prepared foods section.

A There are many kinds of loaves of bread. A small loaf is sliced into 8 slices. If Noah buys 2 small loaves, how many slices will he have altogether?
(10 points for the math sentence, 10 points for the answer)

Math Sentence

Answer ( )

B He looked for packs of dinner rolls. He found dinner rolls that came in packs of 6. When there are 5 packs, how many rolls are there altogether?
(10 points for the math sentence, 10 points for the answer)

Math Sentence

Answer ( )

C Noah found pizzas in the prepared foods section. A whole pizza is divided into 8 slices. When there are 6 whole pizzas, how many slices of pizza are there altogether?
(10 points for the math sentence, 10 points for the answer)

Math Sentence

Answer ( )

D Noah also likes fried chicken. There are 9 pieces of fried chicken in a box. If he buys 2 boxes, how many pieces of fried chicken will he take home?
(10 points for the math sentence, 10 points for the answer)

Math Sentence

Answer ( )

E There are 7 pieces of sushi in a package. When there are 4 packages, how many pieces of sushi are there altogether?
(10 points for the math sentence, 10 points for the answer)

Math Sentence

Answer ( )

Date

Score

/100

1 Orion and Aurora are going to observe stars in the summer sky. On the way, they bought special packs of bubble gum. Each pack of gum holds 7 sticks.

A When they buy 2 packs, how many sticks are there altogether?
(15 points for the math sentence, 10 points for the answer)

Math Sentence

Answer ( )

B When they don't buy any gum, how many sticks of gum do they have?
(15 points for the math sentence, 10 points for the answer)

Math Sentence

Answer ( )

To think about the math sentence for **B**, you should think of "they don't buy any gum" as "buying zero gum."

40

2 Each stick of gum is worth points that Orion and Aurora can use for rewards.
When customers reach 10 points, they will get a gift reward.

Ⓐ One pack had 4 sticks, and each was worth 2 points. How many points did they get altogether? (15 points for the math sentence, 10 points for the answer)

Math Sentence

Answer ( )

Ⓑ Another pack had 3 sticks, and each was worth 0 points. How many points did they get altogether? (15 points for the math sentence, 10 points for the answer)

Math Sentence

Answer ( )

Even if there are many 0-point sticks, you will not get any points.
When you put numbers in △ of the sentence 0 × △ (such as, 0 × 1, 0 × 3, 0 × 10), the answer will always be 0.

19 Multiplication – Star Gazing (Part 2)

Date . .

Score / 100

1 Aurora is counting stars in the sky.

Ⓐ She counts stars by making groups of 6 stars. When she finds 9 groups, how many stars has she counted altogether?
(10 points for the math sentence, 10 points for the answer)

Math Sentence

Answer (   )

Ⓑ When she finds 10 groups, how many stars has she counted altogether? Write an addition sentence by using the answer to problem Ⓐ.
(10 points for the math sentence, 10 points for the answer)

Math Sentence

Answer (   )

Ⓒ When she finds 11 groups, how many stars has she counted altogether? Write an addition sentence by using the answer to problem Ⓑ.
(10 points for the math sentence, 10 points for the answer)

Math Sentence

Answer (   )

2 Orion used multiplication to find answers to the same problems above.

A He counts stars by making a group of 6 stars. When he finds 10 groups, how many stars are there altogether? Write a math sentence using multiplication.
(10 points for the math sentence, 10 points for the answer)

Math Sentence

Answer $\left($ $\right)$

B When he finds 11 groups, how many stars are there altogether? Write a math sentence using multiplication. (10 points for the math sentence, 10 points for the answer)

Math Sentence

Answer $\left($ $\right)$

Aurora found the number of stars by solving $54 + 6$ and $60 + 6$. This is the same as $6 \times 9 + 6$ and $6 \times 10 + 6$.

Orion found the answer by using 6×10 and 6×11.

$6 \times 9 + 6$ is the same as 6×10 and $6 \times 10 + 6$ is the same as 6×11.

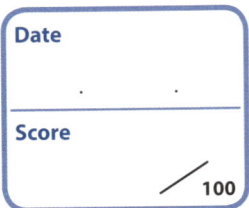

Date

Score

/100

1 Katia likes to play cards with her friends. She is thinking about making math problems using the cards.

A A dealer (the person who distributes cards) gave 5 cards each to 4 players. How many cards did the dealer distribute altogether?
(10 points for the math sentence, 10 points for the answer)

Answer ( )

B Then the dealer distributed 3 more cards to each of the 4 players. How many cards did the dealer distribute altogether?
(10 points for the math sentence, 10 points for the answer)

Math Sentence

Answer ( )

In problem **B**, you can think about the total number of cards the dealer distributed to each player. Then figure out the total number of cards distributed to all the players.

We could also find the total number of cards the dealer distributed to all players the first and second time separately. Then add these two numbers together.

2 A deck of playing card has four different suits called spades (♠), hearts (♥), diamonds (♦), and clubs (♣). Each suit has ten number cards from 1 to 10 and three face cards called the king, queen, and jack. In addition to number and face cards, a deck of cards usually comes with two joker cards.

A How many face cards are there altogether in a deck of cards? Calculate and write a number sentence. (10 points for the math sentence, 10 points for the answer)

Math Sentence

Answer ( )

B How many red face cards are there in a deck of cards? (20 points)

Math Sentence

Answer ( )

 **C** How many cards are there in a deck of cards after the jokers are removed? Calculate and write a math sentence. (10 points for the math sentence, 10 points for the answer)

Math Sentence

Answer ( )

Each suit has the same number of cards.

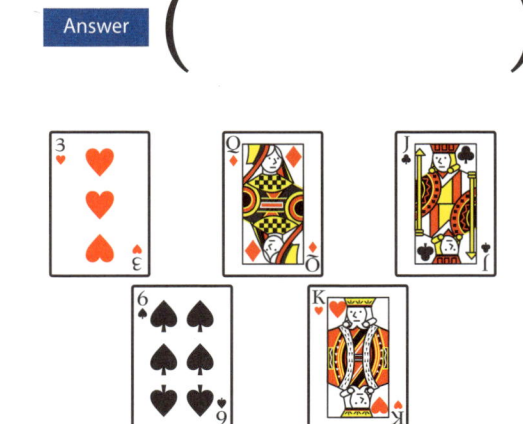

45

Game Rules

① Each player picks one card from a deck of cards that are face down.
② Calculate points based on the card each person gets.

If the card is a spade (♠), multiply the number on the card 3 times.
If the card is a club (♣), multiply the number on the card 4 times.
If the card is a diamond (♦), multiply the number on the card 5 times.
If the card is a heart (♥), multiply the number on the card 6 times.

Example

Number on the card	Suit	Calculation	Score
2	♠	$2 \times 3 = 6$	6 points
3	♦	$3 \times 5 = 15$	15 points
4	♥	$4 \times 6 = 24$	24 points

1 Put appropriate numbers in the ☐ in the table below. Then calculate the scores.
(5 points each for both the math sentence and the score)

Number on the card	Suit	Calculation	Score
7	♣	$7 \times \boxed{} = \boxed{}$	☐ points
9	♦	$\boxed{} \times \boxed{} = \boxed{}$	☐ points
10	♥	$\boxed{} \times \boxed{} = \boxed{}$	☐ points
13	♠	$\boxed{} \times \boxed{} = \boxed{}$	☐ points

2 Katia and Jose are playing this card game.

A Put appropriate numbers in the ☐ in the table below. Then, calculate their scores.
(5 points each for both the math sentence and the score)

1st game

	Number on the card	Suit	Calculation	Score
Katia	7	♠	☐ × ☐ = ☐	☐ points
Jose	10	♦	☐ × ☐ = ☐	☐ points

2nd game

	Number on the card	Suit	Calculation	Score
Katia	9	♥	☐ × ☐ = ☐	☐ points
Jose	6	♣	☐ × ☐ = ☐	☐ points

B How many total points did Jose get from the first and the second game?
(10 points for the math sentence, 10 points for the answer)

Math Sentence

Answer ☐ points

C Katia and Jose played one more game. Jose's total score is now 116. How many points did he get in the third game?
(10 points for the math sentence, 10 points for the answer)

Math Sentence

Answer ☐ points

D What card did Jose get in the third game? Put the number of the card in the ☐, then circle the suit of the card. (10 points for the number, 10 points for the suit)

Number ☐   Suit ♠ ♣ ♦ ♥

47

Date

Score

/100

1 Calculate the following division problems. (5 points each)

(A) 35 ÷ 5

(B) 9 ÷ 3

(C) 18 ÷ 9

(D) 24 ÷ 6

(E) 14 ÷ 2

(F) 48 ÷ 8

(G) 42 ÷ 7

(H) 27 ÷ 9

(I) 21 ÷ 3

(J) 9 ÷ 9

(K) 0 ÷ 6

(L) 0 ÷ 8

2 Calculate the following division problems. (5 points each)

(A) 14 ÷ 1

(B) 0 ÷ 20

(C) 30 ÷ 30

(D) 36 ÷ 1

If the dividend or the divisor is a large number, you can solve the problem in the same way as problem **1**.

3 Read the math problems below. Which problems require the math sentence 9 ÷ 3 to solve? Write the letter for each of the problems that can be solved by 9 ÷ 3. (10 points)

    A. There are 9 children. 3 apples are given to each child. How many apples were given out?

    B. There are 9 ballpoint pens. When each person gets 3 ballpoint pens, how many people will get pens?

    C. There are 3 bags of 9 candies. How many candies are there altogether?

    D. There are 9 chocolates. After you eat 3 of them, how many chocolates are left?

    E. 9 students will be separated into 3 teams equally. How many students are there on each team?

(   )

If you can solve this, the math - *and you* - are cool!

Read problems A to E carefully. Think about the math sentence that represents each problem.

4 Write a word problem that can be solved by 30 ÷ 5. (10 points)

1 Calculate the following. (6 points each)

A 30 ÷ 3

B 80 ÷ 8

C 45 ÷ 3

D 52 ÷ 4

E 72 ÷ 6

F 96 ÷ 8

For problems A and B, think about making groups of 10s.
For problem C, think about decomposing 45 into 30 and 15.
For problems D to F, think about decomposing the dividend into tens that are divisible by the divisor, and what is left.

2 Calculate the following. (6 points each)

A 200 ÷ 4

B 500 ÷ 5

C 800 ÷ 4

D 900 ÷ 3

When dividing hundreds, think about making groups of hundreds and tens.

3 Answer the following questions.

A Find the answer to $56 \div 14$ by putting appropriate numbers in the $①$ through $⑤$. (6 points each)

The answer to $56 \div 14$ is equal to the number that goes into the box of the multiplication sentence below.

$$14 \times \boxed{} = 56$$

Let's think about how to find the appropriate number for the box above.

$$14 \times \boxed{1} = \boxed{①}$$

$$14 \times \boxed{2} = \boxed{②}$$

$$14 \times \boxed{3} = \boxed{③}$$

$$14 \times \boxed{4} = \boxed{④}$$

So,

$$56 \div 14 = \boxed{⑤}$$

B Think about how to calculate $65 \div 13$ using the strategy learned and applied in problem **A**. (5 points)

( )

C Find the answer to $96 \div 24$ using the strategy learned above. (5 points)

( )

51

Date

.   .

Score

/100

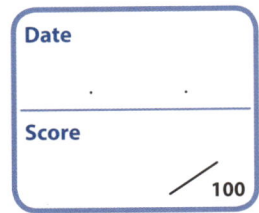

1 In mathematics classes, students use counters to think about and solve problems. Takanobu likes math and he is so excited to solve more problems.

Ⓐ There are 32 students in Takanobu's class. They are divided into 4 equal groups. How many students are there in one group?
(10 points for the math sentence, 10 points for the answer)

Math Sentence

Answer ( )

Ⓑ Mr. Tanner, Takanobu's teacher, had 800 counters in his math supply closet. Takanobu's classmates were surprised to see such a large number of counters. At the beginning of the first math class, Mr. Tanner asked the students to divide the counters into four bags equally. How many counters will there be in each bag?
(10 points for the math sentence, 10 points for the answer)

Math Sentence

Answer ( )

How many groups of 100 are there in 800?

2 Mr. Tanner gave a math problem using counters to his students. Read the dialogue below and answer questions **A** and **B**.

Mr. Tanner : Make and fill in a square that has 6 counters per side.

Takanobu : I wonder what kind of math problem we are going to solve. I can't wait to solve it!

David : Yeah!

Mr. Tanner : Now, you will make and fill in a rectangle by changing the height of the square and keeping the total number of counters the same.
How many counters will make up the bottom row of the rectangle? See if you can think about and solve this problem without using counters.

A If they change the height of the rectangle to 4 counters, how many counters will make up the bottom row? (15 points for the math sentence, 15 points for the answer)

Math Sentence

Answer ( )

B If they change the height of the rectangle to 3 counters, how many counters will make up the bottom row? (15 points for the math sentence, 15 points for the answer)

Math Sentence

Answer ( )

1 Nashita and Chang's family and friends are camping at Green Forest and River Campground. There are 52 campers altogether. Nashita and Chang have been looking forward to this camping trip for a long time. They know they will have many happy memories at the end of this summer vacation.

A They are putting up the tents now. Each tent can sleep 6 people. How many tents do they need to put up, so everyone can sleep in a tent?
(10 points for the math sentence, 10 points for the answer)

Math Sentence

Answer ( )

B Everyone went fishing at the river. 15 people caught trout. 25 people caught catfish. There were 5 people who caught both trout and catfish. Fill in cells ① through ⑨ of the following table with appropriate numbers. (5 points each)

		Number of People Who Caught Trout		
		Yes	No	Total
Number of People Who Caught Catfish	Yes	①	②	③
	No	④	⑤	⑥
	Total	⑦	⑧	⑨

54

C The following diagram shows the connections between the people who went fishing. The diagram shows 4 areas; A, B, C, and D.

The shaded area A shows the number of people who caught both trout and catfish. As stated in problem **B**, 5 will be the number in shaded area A.

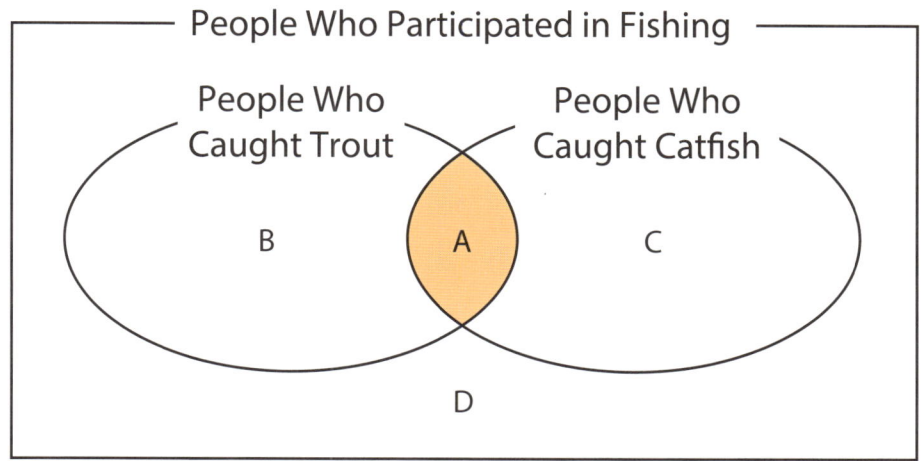

People Who Participated in Fishing

People Who Caught Trout

People Who Caught Catfish

B   A   C

D

Think about what group is represented in areas B, C, and D. Then use the numbers from problem **B** to fill in the number of people belonging in each area of the diagram. (10 points for B and C, 15 points for D)

B (   )   C (   )   D (   )

The diagram shown in problem **B** is called a Venn Diagram.
Each circle represents a specific condition or group (set).
The overlapping part represents a group that meets both of the two conditions.
The area outside these circles represents the group that does not meet either condition.

55

1 Nashita and Chang love to go camping. They are so excited about finding many different insects. They counted the number of insects they saw at camp and created the graph below.

Number of Insects Found Near Our Campsite

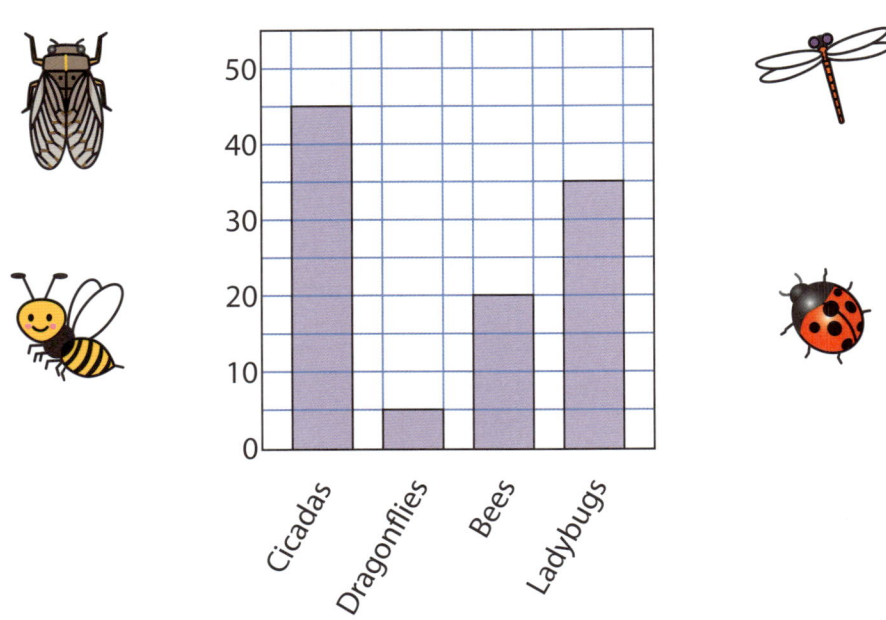

A What is the difference between the number of cicadas and the number of bees? (10 points for the math sentence, 10 points for the answer)

Math Sentence

Answer ( )

B How many times as many ladybugs did they see as dragonflies? (20 points)

Math Sentence

Answer ( )

56

If you can solve this, the math - *and you* - are cool!

Drawing a graph helps us to compare the difference between two quantities easily. If you can record data and summarize it using a graph, just as Nashita and Chang did, the math-*and you*-are cool!

C Cicadas, dragonflies, bees and ladybugs are insects. This means they all have 6 legs. If we count all the legs on all the insects that Nashita and Chang found, how many legs would there be altogether?

(15 points for the math sentence, 15 points for the answer)

Math Sentence

Answer ( )

2 In the evening, Nashita and Chang enjoyed having a barbecue with friends and family. After dinner they ate watermelon. Nashita and Chang were smiling because the watermelon was so sweet and delicious. One of the watermelons weighed 2 kg. Nashita ate 600 g of it. Chang ate 300 g more than Nashita.
How many grams of watermelon is left now?
(15 points for the math sentence, 15 points for the answer)

Math Sentence

Answer ( )

Date

.   .

Score

/100

1 Mr. Tanner placed many counters to make the square shape shown below.

Mr. Tanner asked his students, "How many counters are there altogether? There are so many counters, it is hard to count them all one-by-one. Do you have any good ideas to count them easily?"

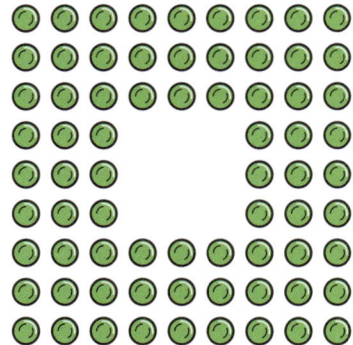

Takanobu and his group tried to find the best solution. They came up with three solutions as shown in **A** to **C** below. Could you figure out how they solved the problem? Check their work and use math sentences to show their method. Then, the math sentences will help you find the number of counters.

A Takanobu's solution

I found the sum of the counters by dividing them into 8 groups. Each group has an equal number of counters, as shown to the right.
(15 points for the math sentence, 15 points for the answer)

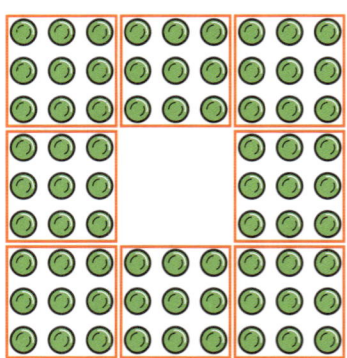

Math Sentence

Answer (   )

B  Elle's solution

I found the sum of the counters by placing counters in the empty space in the middle of the square, as shown to the right. (15 points for the math sentence, 15 points for the answer)

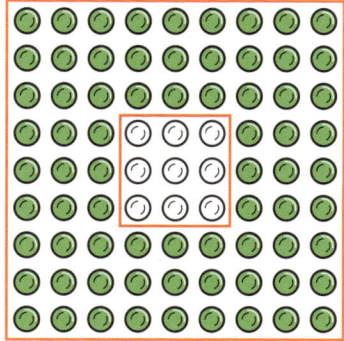

Math Sentence

Answer ( )

In problem **B**, you may subtract the number of counters in the in the middle, small square from the sum of the counters in the larger square.

C  Mario's solution

I found the sum of the counters by making 4 groups each with an equal number of counters, as shown on the right. (20 points for the math sentence, 20 points for the answer)

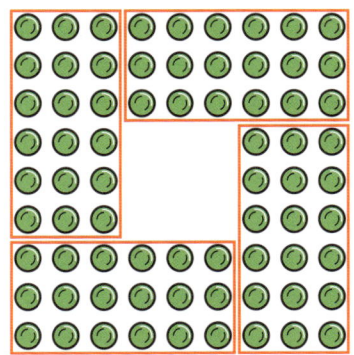

Math Sentence

Answer ( )

28 **Let's Plant Trees and Flowers! (Part 1)**

Date

Score

/ 100

1 There is a straight road leading to Zoom-Up Elementary School. This road is 56 meters long. There are 8 trees planted along this road. There is an equal distance between each tree. Mr. Green and Teddy are talking about a way to find the distance between the trees.

Ⓐ Read the dialogue below and put the appropriate number in the ☐ below. (20 points)

Mr. Green : How many meters are between the trees?

Teddy : The length of the road is 56 m and there are 8 trees. So, 56 ÷ 8 = 7 m.

Mr. Green : It is correct to use division. But you are finding the distance between the trees so you must count the number of spaces between the trees, not the number of trees. Look at the picture below and count how many spaces there are.

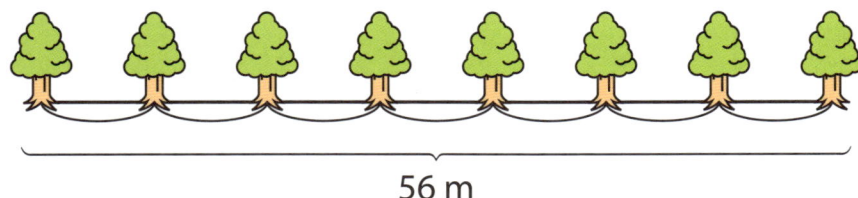

56 m

Teddy : The number of spaces between the trees is ☐ .

Mr. Green : That's right. Now, what is the distance between the trees in meters?

Teddy : Mr. Green, now I understand how to solve the problem!

Ⓑ Refer to the dialogue above. What is the distance between the trees in meters? (10 points for the math sentence, 10 points for the answer)

Math Sentence

Answer ( )

60

2 In April, many tulips bloom in the garden of Zoom-Up Elementary School. Teddy likes to visit the flower beds and see the colorful flowers with their beautiful green leaves.

His 3rd grade classmates decided to plant sunflower seeds in a flower bed that is 8 m long. They want to plant seeds from one end of the flower bed to the other end, and keep 10 cm of space between each seed.

How many sunflower seeds do they need altogether?

Put appropriate numbers in the ☐ below. (10 points each)

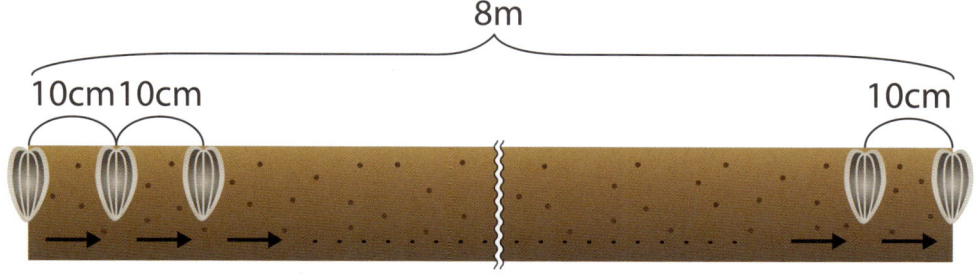

The flower bed is measured in meters (m). The distance between seeds is measured in centimeters (cm). It isn't easy to calculate when the units are different. So, make the units the same.

Convert 8 m into cm:

$$8 \text{ m} = \boxed{①} \text{ cm}$$

Then, find the number of spaces between seeds.

Remember that students want to plant seeds from one edge to the other with 10 cm spaces between each seed.

So, the number of spaces between seeds is:

$$\boxed{②} \div \boxed{③} = \boxed{④}$$

The number of seeds is $\boxed{⑤}$ more than the number of spaces between seeds.

So, students will need $\boxed{⑥}$ seeds altogether.

> Problem ⑤ is difficult. So, you need to recall what we thought about when we looked at the diagram in problem **1**. In that problem, we compared the number of trees and the number of spaces between the trees!

29 **Let's Plant Trees and Flowers! (Part 2)**

Date

. .

Score

/100

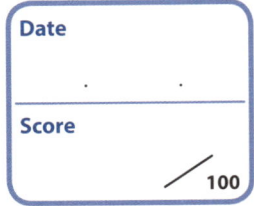

1 There are many koi fish in the pond at Zoom-Up Elementary School. The shape of the pond is a circle and the circumference (length around the circle) is 48 m.
Teddy is hoping that the school will put some plants around the pond. He told Mr. Green about his idea to plant flowers around the pond. Mr. Green said "I have some flowers in my garden at home. I will bring them to school and we can plant them together!" Teddy is so excited about that.

A They decide to plant flowers every 4 m around the pond.
How many spaces will there be between the flowers?
(20 points for the math sentence, 20 points for the answer)

4 m

Math Sentence

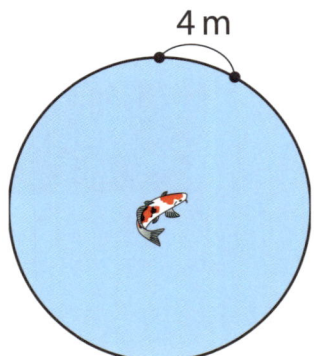

Answer ( )

B In problem **A**, how many flowers will they need? (20 points)

( )

Think about the relationship between the number of flowers and the number of spaces between the flowers.
There is no end point in the circumference around the pond.
So this problem is different from the previous problem, where the trees were planted along a straight road.
Please think carefully!

C Mr. Green wanted to plant the number of flowers they discussed in problem B, but there are only 8 flowers in his garden. So, he and Teddy decide to plant the 8 flowers around the pond. They make sure they have equal spaces between each flower. How many meters are between each flower?

(20 points for the math sentence, 20 points for the answer)

Math Sentence

Answer ( )

If you can solve this, the math - *and you* - are cool!

It is easier to think about problem C by drawing a diagram that shows how 8 flowers are planted and the space between each flower. This way, you can easily figure out the number of spaces between the flowers. Drawing diagrams is an important way to help you think about difficult problems. If you develop the skill of drawing diagrams on your own, then you will be able to solve challenging problems. The math, and your thinking, will be cool!

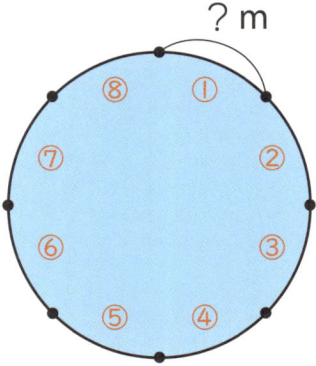

1 What fraction of the whole circle is represented by the shaded part? Answer the following with fraction notation. (5 points for each ☐)

A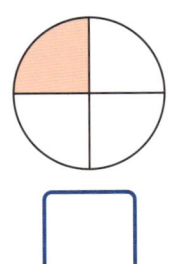

B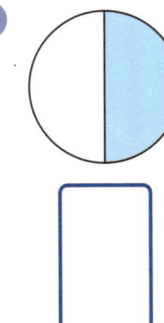

C

2 Look at the diagram and put appropriate numbers in the ☐ below. (5 points)

$\frac{1}{2}$

$\frac{1}{8}$

When you put together ☐ $\frac{1}{8}$s, it will be equal to $\frac{1}{2}$.

3 Color the part that represents $\frac{1}{4}$ of each square. (10 points each)

A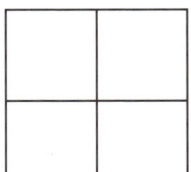

B

C

4 Put appropriate numbers in the ☐ below. (10 points for each ☐)

When you put together ☐ $\frac{1}{2}$ apples, it will equal a whole apple.

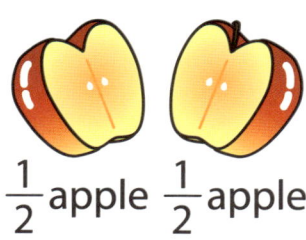

$\frac{1}{2}$ apple $\frac{1}{2}$ apple

When you put together four ☐ apples, it will equal a whole apple.

5 What is the fraction of the square that is represented by the shaded part?
Answer the following with fraction notation. (10 points for each ☐)

Ⓐ
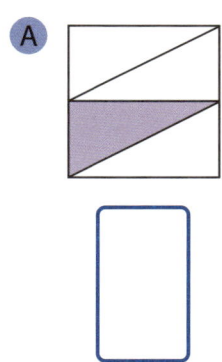
☐

Ⓑ
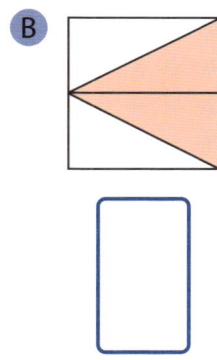
☐

Ⓒ
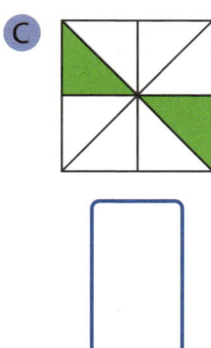
☐

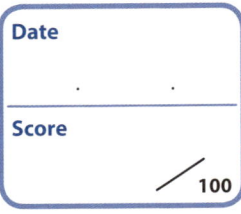

Date

Score

/100

1 Put appropriate numbers in the ☐ below. (8 points each)

Ⓐ The number that is made of six ☐ s is $\frac{6}{7}$.

Ⓑ The volume $\frac{3}{8}$ L is composed of 3 of a volume that is composed of 1L divided into ☐ equal parts.

Ⓒ The length $\frac{5}{6}$ m is composed of ☐ lengths that are equal to 1m divided into 6 equal parts.

2 There are two tapes A and B.

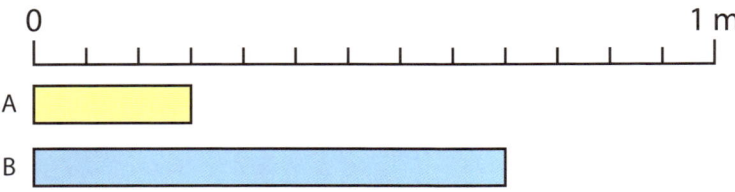

Ⓐ How many meters is the length of tape B? Show your answer in a fraction. (8 points)

(m)

🖐 Ⓑ How many times longer is tape B than tape A? (8 points)

(times)

3 Compare each pair of two fractions. Then write the appropriate inequality sign (> or <) in the ☐ below. (7 points each)

Ⓐ $\dfrac{3}{7}\ \boxed{}\ \dfrac{5}{7}$

Ⓑ $\dfrac{7}{9}\ \boxed{}\ \dfrac{5}{9}$

4 Put appropriate numbers in the ☐ below. (8 points each)

Ⓐ The fraction $\dfrac{3}{8}$ is $\boxed{}$ smaller than 1.

Ⓑ 1 is $\boxed{}$ larger than $\dfrac{4}{7}$.

5 Order the following numbers from the least to the greatest. (10 points each)

Ⓐ $\dfrac{3}{8},\ \dfrac{1}{8},\ \dfrac{6}{8},\ \dfrac{5}{8}$

(   )

Ⓑ $\dfrac{2}{9},\ 1,\ \dfrac{5}{9},\ \dfrac{4}{9}$

(   )

Ⓒ $\dfrac{1}{4},\ \dfrac{1}{3},\ \dfrac{1}{5},\ \dfrac{1}{10}$

(   )

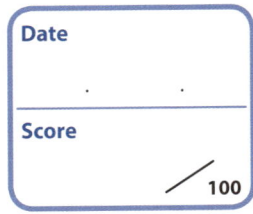

Date . .

Score / 100

1 A rabbit named Robert and a turtle named Tomy want to participate in a race. The goal is to get to Wonderland Park first. Now the race starts! Ready, set, go!

A Robert runs 30 minutes, then he runs another 50 minutes. How many hours and minutes has he run? (15 points)

Answer ( )

B 1 hour and 10 minutes has passed since Tomy started the race. He stopped one time to rest 20 minutes during the run. How many minutes has he run so far? (15 points)

Answer ( )

C Robert ran 1 hour. Tomy ran 90 minutes. Who ran longer? How many minutes longer? (20 points)

Answer ( )

You can convert 1 hour into 60 minutes, can't you?

D It took 40 minutes for Tomy to run from Wonderland bridge to the top of the next hill. He arrived at the top of the hill at 10:50. What time was it when he was at the bridge? (15 points)

Answer ( )

E After Tomy reached the top of the hill at 10:50, he ran another 20 minutes to get to the observatory. What time did he arrive at the observatory? (15 points)

Answer ( )

F Robert passed Wonderland bridge at 8:56 and arrived at the top of the hill 20 minutes later. What time did he arrive at the top of the hill? (20 points)

Answer ( )

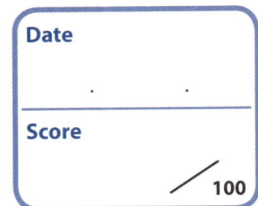

1 Robert, the rabbit, has pulled far ahead of Tomy, the turtle. I wonder what will happen next in the race.

A Robert arrived at a carrot field at 9:30. He was so hungry, he decided to eat carrots for a snack. He spent 80 minutes eating carrots! What time did he finish his snack? (20 points)

Answer ( )

It is a good idea to convert 80 minutes into hours and minutes.

You might want to think about the time it takes to get to 10:00 first.

B Tomy passed in front of a temple 70 minutes ago. It is 2:20 now. What time did he pass in front of the temple? (20 points)

Answer ( )

C The race started at 7:30 a.m.. How many hours and minutes will pass until 1:00 p.m.?
(20 points)

Answer ( )

D Robert got sleepy after his snack. So, he decided to take a nap for a short time. He fell
asleep at 11:00 a.m. and he got up 4 hours later! What time did he get up?
Answer using "a.m." or "p.m.". (20 points)

Answer ( )

E Tomy arrived at Wonderland Park at 3:30 p.m.. Robert, the rabbit, arrived there
40 minutes after he got up from his nap. Who arrived at Wonderland Park first,
Robert or Tomy? How many minutes earlier did the winner cross the finishing line?
(20 points)

Answer ( )

You can find the time that Robert got up by
using the result of problem D. Think about
what time Robert arrived at the goal.

71

34

Time and Elapsed Time

Date

.   .

Score

/100

1 Put appropriate numbers in the ☐ below. (10 points each)

A   3 minutes = ☐ seconds

B   85 seconds = ☐ minute ☐ seconds

C   ☐ seconds = 1 minute 10 seconds

D   305 seconds = ☐ minutes ☐ seconds

E   ☐ seconds = 3 minutes 40 seconds

2 Put the following times A to F in order from shortest to longest. (10 points)

A. 8 minutes   B. 600 seconds

C. 1 hour   D. 3 minutes

E. 12 minutes   F. 300 seconds

(☐ → ☐ → ☐ → ☐ → ☐ → ☐)

If you convert A - F into minutes, you will be able to compare the times easily!

 **3** Calculate the following. (10 points each)

A
      1 hour 50 minutes

 + 4 hours 20 minutes
_____

B
     24 minutes 25 seconds

 − 17 minutes 38 seconds
_____

C
     1 day 6 hours 32 minutes 14 seconds

 +   10 hours 36 minutes 45 seconds
_____

 1 hour = 60 minutes and 1 minute = 60 seconds.
When the sum of minutes or seconds is over 60,
regroup to add 1 to the higher unit.

4 Teddy took 73 seconds to solve three calculation problems.
Naomi took 1 minute 8 seconds to solve the same problems.
Who solved the problems faster? How many seconds faster was that
person? (10 points)

(solved the problems   seconds faster than   )

35

School-Related Math Problems

Date

.   .

Score

/100

1 Benjamin is thinking about occasions when he uses mathematics at school. He decides to record these occasions in his notebook.

A Benjamin got up at 6:45 a.m. The morning assembly will begin at 9:00 a.m. How many hours and minutes will pass before the assembly begins? (20 points)

(   )

B The principal of Benjamin's school said that the school has 368 boys and 409 girls. How many students are there altogether?
(10 points for the math sentence, 10 points for the answer)

Math Sentence

Answer (   )

C How many fewer boys are there than girls?
(10 points for the math sentence, 10 points for the answer)

Math Sentence

Answer (   )

2 Benjamin and Greg played a card game after lunch. Each card has a number on it. The deck of cards includes only cards with the numbers 0, 2, 5, 8 and 10. Each boy took turns drawing a card from the deck. The number on each card gives the player that number of points. The final score will be calculated by finding the total points after each boy picks 20 cards.

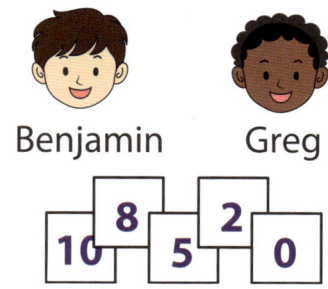

Benjamin   Greg

Benjamin is very competitive, so he really wants to win!
The table below shows the results of the game.

The number on the card picked	The number of cards Benjamin picked	The number of cards Greg picked
10	0	3
8	9	2
5	7	10
2	1	5
0	3	0

Ⓐ How many points did Benjamin have altogether?
(10 points for the math sentence, 10 points for the answer)

Math Sentence

Answer (　　　　)

Ⓑ The player who gets the most points wins. Who is the winner, Benjamin or Greg?
(20 points)

(　　)

75

36

Going to Zoom-Up Park

Date

.   .

Score

/100

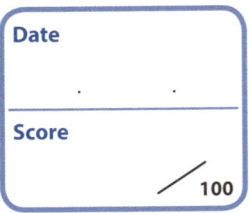

1 Zoom-Up Park is famous for beautiful flowers and trees. Many people visit the park to enjoy nature and relax.

Jada and her family are planning to go to the park this coming Saturday. They are thinking about taking a bus to the park.

The table to the right shows the bus schedule at the bus stop near Jada's house between the hours of 9:00 a.m. and 1:00 p.m.

Hour	Minute			
9 AM	7	27	47	
10 AM	7	27	47	
11 AM	5	20	35	50
12 PM	5	20	35	50
1 PM	7	27	47	

A How many minutes are there between the 10:47 a.m. bus and the next bus? (20 points)

(   )

B Jada's family gets to the bus stop at 12:26 p.m. They are going to take the next bus. How many minutes will they need to wait? (20 points)

(   )

C It takes 48 minutes to go to Zoom-Up Park by bus. Given the information in problem **B**, what time will Jada's family arrive at the park? (20 points)

(   )

Did you figure out how to read and use the bus schedule? When you take a trip with your family or friends, create a trip plan using a bus schedule. If you can take charge and help others plan a trip, it will be so cool!

2 There were many pink and white cherry blossoms in full bloom at Zoom-Up Park. Jada collected the beautiful blossoms that had fallen to the ground. Then, Jada arranged the pink and white blossoms as shown here in the picture. How many blossoms are there altogether?
(10 points for the math sentence, 10 points for the answer)

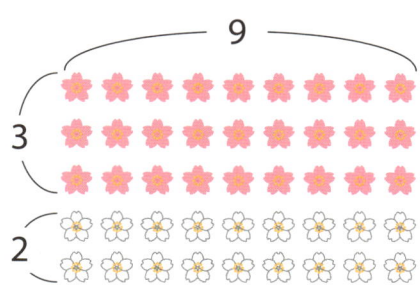

Math Sentence

Answer ( )

3 Jada was so thirsty at the park. She and her mother decided to go to the store to buy some drinks. There was a sign in the store window announcing that drinks were on sale. The sign is shown below.

> Buy 5 drinks, 50 cents off!
>
> Buy 10 drinks, 1 dollar 50 cents off!

Jada bought 5 cans of fruit drinks that were priced 2 dollars each. How much did she pay altogether?
(10 points for the math sentence, 10 points for the answer)

Math Sentence

Answer ( )

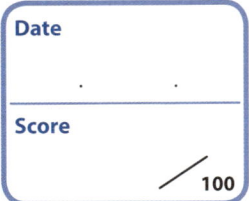

Date

Score
/100

1 The 3rd grade students of Zoom-Up Elementary School are going on a field trip to the Sweet Factory next Tuesday. The students are so excited about the field trip! They are planning to take a 9:36 a.m. bus from the stop near the school. The bus will arrive at a bus stop near the factory at 11:28 a.m. How long will the bus ride to the factory be? (20 points)

(   )

2 The Sweet Factory produces many kinds of sweets. Miles and Shanika enjoy looking at how the sweets are produced. They want to know how many sweets are made at the factory. So, they asked the factory guide. They summarized what they learned in their notebook shown below.

Numbers of Sweets Produced Yesterday

Chocolates	Cookies	Candies
12,040	10 times more than chocolates	100 times more than chocolates

A How many cookies were made yesterday? Write the answer number in word form. (10 points for the math sentence, 10 points for the answer)

Math Sentence

Answer (cookies)

78

B How many candies were made yesterday? Write the answer number in word form. (15 points for the math sentence, 15 points for the answer)

Math Sentence

Answer (candies)

C How many more cookies than chocolates were made yesterday? Write the answer number in word form. (15 points for the math sentence, 15 points for the answer)

Math Sentence

Answer (cookies)

Large numbers with many zeros!

You will learn about larger numbers than 1,000 in Grade 4 and higher.

When you have a large number with six zeros…
1,000,000 　　　　　　　　　　　　it is 1 million.

When you have a large number with nine zeros…
1,000,000,000 　　　　　　　　　　it is 1billion.

When you have a large number with twelve zeros…
1,000,000,000,000 　　　　　　　　it is 1 trillion.

When you have a large number with fifteen zeros…
1,000,000,000,000,000 　　　　　　it is 1 quadrillion.

When you have a large number with eighteen zeros…
1,000,000,000,000,000,000 　　　　it is 1 quintillion.

When you have a large number with twenty-one zeros…
1,000,000,000,000,000,000,000 　　it is 1 sextillion.

It is too easy to make mistakes or lose track when writing so many zeros to express numbers as large as these! So these numbers are often written in a shorter form. For example, 1 billion with 9 zeros is written as 10^9 (10 to the 9th power) and 1 trillion with 12 zeros is written as 10^{12} (10 to the 12th power). Don't you agree this is a brilliant idea to show such large numbers?

A challenge for you: Why don't you find the names of large numbers that have more than 21 zeros?!

Liquid Volume – On the Farm (Part 1)

Date

Score

/100

1 Mr. Williams owns a farm. He works hard every day to deliver fine quality delicious milk to his customers.

A Farmers start working early in the morning. Farmer Williams has finished milking two cows, Buttercup and Bovinea. He milked 2 L 400 mL from Buttercup and 5 L 500 mL from Bovinea. How much milk did he collect this morning?
(10 points for the math sentence, 10 points for the answer)

Math Sentence

Answer ( )

B Which cow produced more milk, Buttercup or Bovinea? How much more milk did she produce?
(10 points for the math sentence, 10 points for the answer)

Math Sentence

Answer ( )

1L (liter) = 1000mL (milliliter)

2 Farmer Williams kept 4 L 700 mL of milk for his family today. The family enjoys having fresh milk to drink.

A The family drank 1 L 900 mL of milk today. How much milk is left?
(10 points for the math sentence, 10 points for the answer)

Math Sentence

Answer ( )

B The next day, Farmer Williams collected 3 L 600 mL of milk. How much milk is there altogether when the leftover milk from the previous day is added?
(10 points for the math sentence, 10 points for the answer)

Math Sentence

Answer ( )

C Farmer Williams is thinking about selling the milk at the town market when the amount of milk produced reaches 7 L. How much more milk does he need to collect?
(10 points for the math sentence, 10 points for the answer)

Math Sentence

Answer ( )

39 Liquid Volume – On the Farm (Part 2)

Date . .

Score /100

1 Clarabelle is the healthiest cow on the Happy Cow farm. She produces delicious milk every day from Monday through Thursday.

	Calculation of Liquid Volume
Monday	3 L 700 mL + 1 L 800 mL
Tuesday	5 L 300 mL – 2 L 400 mL
Wednesday	4 L – 2 L 600 mL
Thursday	1 L 8 dL + 5 dL + 2 L 9 dL

Ⓐ How much milk did Clarabelle produce on Monday?
(10 points for the math sentence, 10 points for the answer)

Math Sentence

Answer ( )

Ⓑ How much milk did Clarabelle produce on Tuesday?
(10 points for the math sentence, 10 points for the answer)

Math Sentence

Answer ( )

Ⓒ How much milk did Clarabelle produce on Wednesday?
(10 points for the math sentence, 10 points for the answer)

Math Sentence

Answer ( )

D How much milk did Clarabelle produce on Thursday?
(10 points for the math sentence, 10 points for the answer)

Math Sentence

Answer ()

E What day of the week from Monday through Thursday did Clarabelle produce the most milk? (20 points)

Math Sentence

Answer ()

You might not have heard of the "deciliter" (dL) unit before. 1dL is equal to 100 mL. I wonder if you can use this information to figure out problems **D** and **E** ?

The Units of Liquid Volume

You learned about the metric liquid units such as the liter (L) and milliliter (mL). In this lesson you also learned about another unit called the deciliter (dL).

The relationship of these liquid volume units is 1 L = 10 dL = 1,000 mL.
1 L is 1,000 times as much as 1 mL, and 1 dL is 100 times as much as 1 mL (1 dL = 100 mL).
Another unit called 1 kiloliter (1 kL) is 1,000 times as much as 1 L (1 kL = 1,000 L).

Similar to liquid volume units, the 1 meter (m) unit of length is 1,000 times as long as 1 millimeter (mm). Also, 1 kilometer (km) is 1,000 times longer than 1m.

The relationship among the liquid volume units in the US customary measurement system is complicated. The fluid ounce (fl oz) is the smallest unit used. The 1 cup (cp) unit equals 8 fl oz. The pint (pt) unit equals 16 fl oz. The quart (qt) unit equals 32 fl oz. The gallon (gal) unit equals 128 fl oz.

1 cp = 8 fl oz,
1 pt = 2 cp = 16 fl oz
1 qt = 2 pt = 4 cp = 32 fl oz
1 gal = 4 qt = 8 pt = 16 cp = 128 fl oz

1 Lisa is a 3rd grade student. She wants to be a pharmacist because she wants to help people get better when they are ill. A pharmacist measures medicine and prepares pills or bottles of medicine for patients.

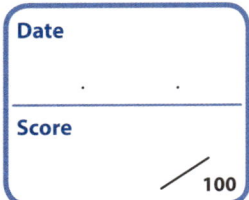

It is important to measure the amount of medicine precisely. If you don't measure precisely, the medicine may not be effective or – even worse – it may harm a patient's body. Lisa is practicing how to measure precisely. She is practicing by using a balance scale to measure weights of salt.

A The balance scale comes with three different weights: a 1 g weight (A), a 4 g weight (B) and an 8 g weight (C). Lisa wants to measure 7 g of salt on the balance scale. First, she puts a different weight on each plate of the balance scale (see the left and right plate on the balance scale). Then, she uses a spoon to add some salt onto the right-side plate. When the weights of both sides balance, she will know the weight of the salt is 7 g. Find which weights Lisa put on each plate of the balance scale. Write A, B or C for each weight below. (10 points each)

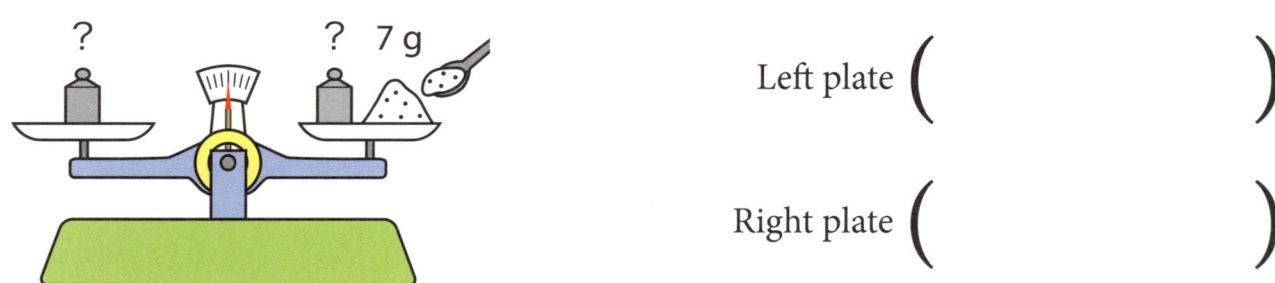

Left plate $\Big($ _____ $\Big)$

Right plate $\Big($ _____ $\Big)$

B Lisa wanted to find out what amounts of weight she could measure using the weights (A), (B), and (C). Each time she measured a weight she used the balance scale only once. She discovered that she could not measure all weights from 1 g through 13 g using the weights she had. List all the weights that she could not measure. (30 points)

$\Big($ _____ $\Big)$

👍 Ⓒ When Lisa was investigating problem Ⓑ, she found that when she used three different weights (other than the 1 g, 4 g, and 8 g weights), she could measure all the weights from 1 g through 13 g and still use the balance scale only once. Find the three different weights that she used. (30 points)

(   )

This is a very difficult problem.
Think about how you can weigh 13 g with 3 weights without using the 1 g, 4 g, and 8 g weights.

2 Now, Lisa is solving balance scale puzzles. There are 5 coins A, B, C, D, and E. All the coins look the same, but only one of them has a different weight than the other coins. Look at the pictures below and find which coin has a different weight. (20 points)

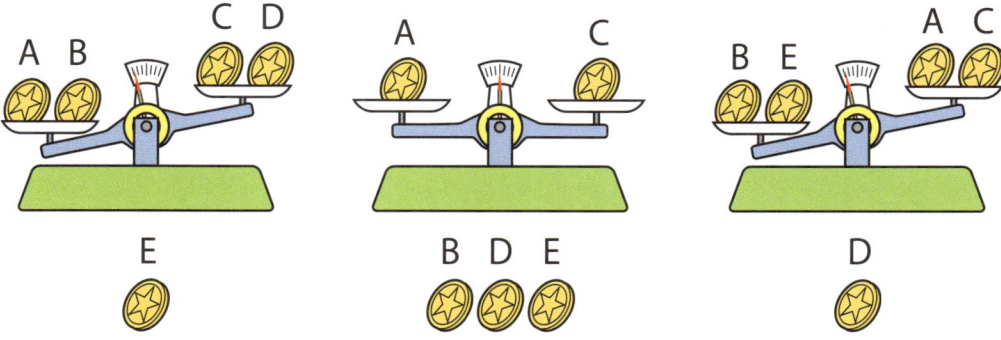

(   )

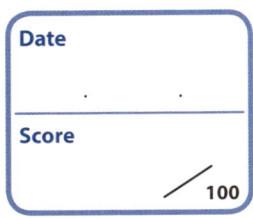
1 Ms. Rice knows Lisa likes the balance scale, so she gave Lisa a balance scale problem to solve.

Ms. Rice : There are 9 coins. They look exactly alike, but one of the coins is heavier than the other coins. Lisa, you want to be a balance scale master, don't you? Can you use a balance scale to figure out which coin is the heavier one?

Lisa : I can find the coin by putting one coin on the left pan, and then check if the other coins have a different weight. I would do this by placing each coin on the right pan one at a time.

Ms. Rice : Yes, you can do that, but you will probably need to use the balance scale several times. I know a way to find the heavier coin by using the balance scale only twice! It works every time.

Lisa : If you can find the coin using the scale only twice, you are awesome!

Ms. Rice : Lisa, can you figure out how to do this?

With Ms. Rice's method, how many coins will be placed on the left and right sides the first time and the second time? (25 points each)

The first time $\left(\right)$

The second time $\left(\right)$

Think about putting 1 coin on each side of the scale, 2 coins on each side of the scale, 3 coins on each side of the scale, and so on.

 **2** Ms. Rice gave one more balance scale puzzle to Lisa.

Ms. Rice : You found the heavy coin. Lisa, you are truly a balance scale master!
Lisa : I'm so happy!
Ms. Rice : I want you to be an even better balance scale master, so I have another problem for you. This is a very challenging problem.
Lisa : I can't wait to solve the problem! I will do my best!

There is a 1 g weight and a 6 g weight. You will measure 40 g of salt using the balance scale and these weights. How many times do you need to use the scale? Find the least number of times you need to use the scale.

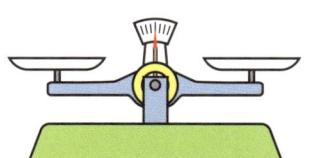

Find the answer of the big challenge above. (50 points)

Answer ( )

After measuring 7 g of salt by using a 1 g weight and a 6 g weight, you can use the salt as a 7 g weight.

91

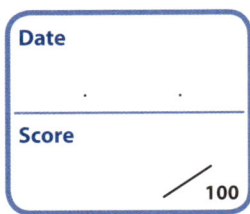

Date

Score

/100

1 Find right angles in the ☐ below. Write the angle's letter in the ☐. (15 points)

Answer ☐

2 Read the text in each ☐ and use a ruler to draw the shapes in the grid spaces below. (15 points each)

Ⓐ A rectangle with sides of 2 cm and 3 cm.

Ⓑ A square with sides of 2 cm.

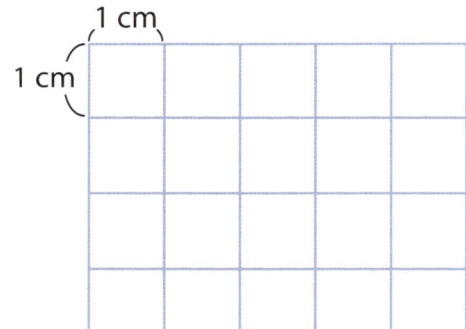

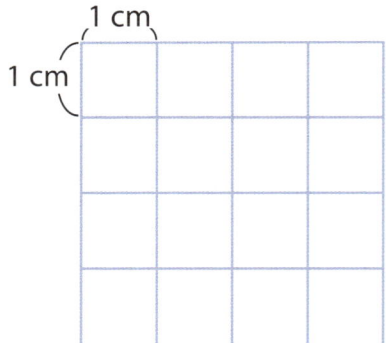

Ⓒ A right triangle with two 2 cm sides that form a right angle.

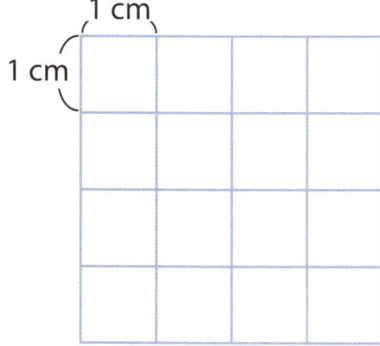

3 There are various shapes drawn on the grid below.

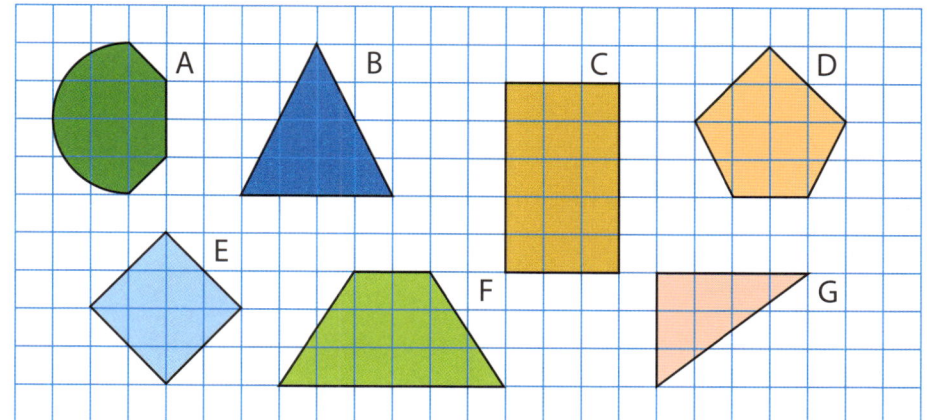

A Find quadrilaterals and write the corresponding letters in the answer box.
(20 points)

Answer [   ]

B Find squares and write the corresponding letters. (10 points)

Answer [   ]

C Find right triangles and write the corresponding letters. (10 points)

Answer [   ]

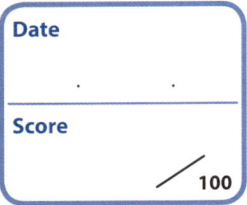

43 Triangles and Quadrilaterals (Part 2)

1 Answer the following questions.

A Measure the length of side A of the square shown below. (5 points)

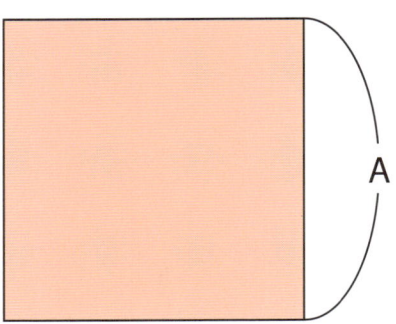

Answer [   ] cm

B How many centimeters (cm) is the perimeter (the sum of the lengths) of the square in problem **A** . (20 points)

Math Sentence

[   ]

Answer [   ] cm

2 There is a triangle that has three equal-length sides. Each side is 7 inches. How many inches (in) is the triangle's perimeter? (25 points)

7 inches

Math Sentence

[   ]

Answer [   ] in

3 There is a rectangle shown here. One of the sides is 4 cm and another side is 2 cm longer than the labeled side.
How many cm is the perimeter? (25 points)

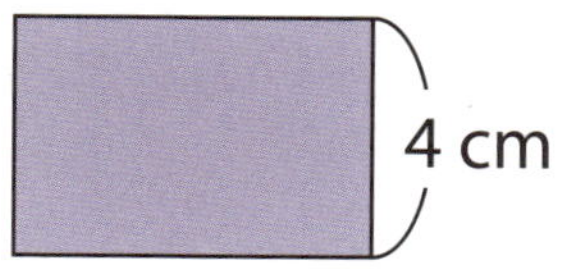

4 cm

Math Sentence

Answer [ ] cm

4 A student measured the sides of a rectangle. The student found a side that was 2 cm 5 mm, and another side was 3 cm 5 mm. How many cm is the rectangle's perimeter? (25 points)

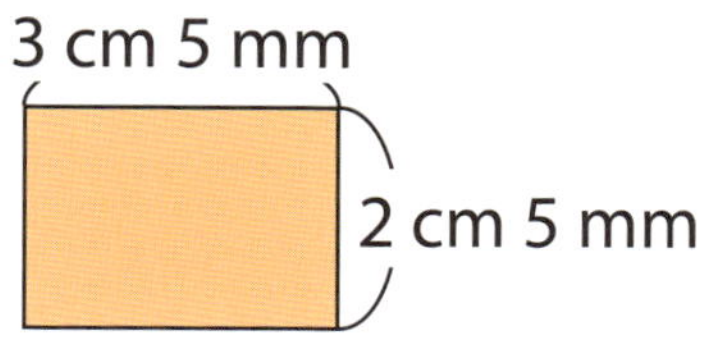

3 cm 5 mm

2 cm 5 mm

Math Sentence

Answer [ ] cm

1 centimeter is 10 millimeters.
1 cm = 10 mm

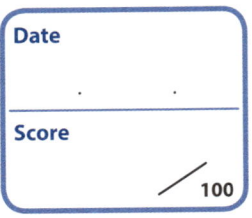

44 Areas (Part 1)

Date

Score ____ /100

1 Find the areas of the shapes below. (15 points)

A

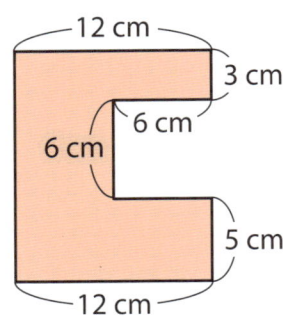

(   )

B

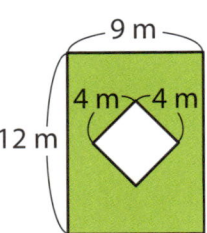

(   )

C

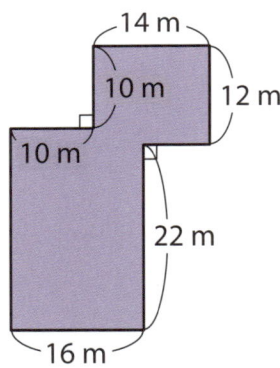

(   )

These shapes are composed of combinations of rectangles and squares.

2 Find the following areas. Record each area using the units shown in each [   ] at the end of each problem statement. (20 points each)

Ⓐ The area of a rectangle with lengths of 5 m and widths of 7 m [cm²]

(   )

Ⓑ The area of a square with sides of 4 yd [ft²]

(   )

3 We connected 4 strips of tape to make the shape shown to the right. Each of the 4 strips of tape measures 20 cm long and 5 cm wide. How many cm² is the area of this large cross shape? (15 points)

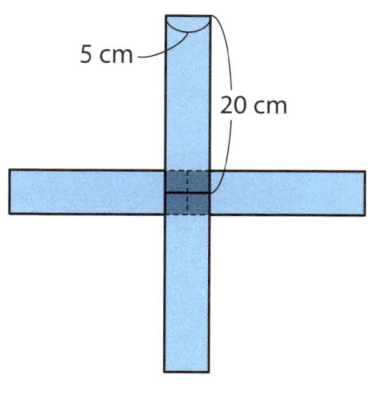

5 cm

20 cm

(   )

If you can solve this, the math - *and you* - are cool!

The darker-shaded part in the drawing is the part where the 4 strips of tape overlap. Think about how to deal with the overlapping part. How many layers of tape overlap at that place?

Date

.   .

Score

/100

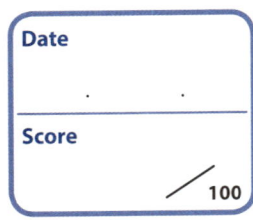

1 There is a rectangle-shaped plot of land that has a length of 30 m and a width of 26 m. The owner is thinking about dividing the land into two parts, A and B as shown below. The area of part B must be 5 times larger than the area of part A. Answer the questions below. (20 points each)

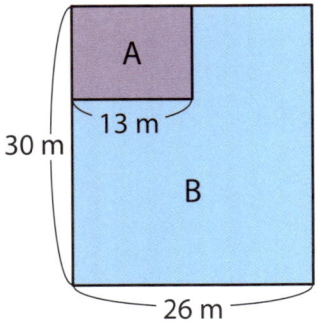

Ⓐ How many m² is the area of the entire plot of land?

( )

Ⓑ How many m² is the area of rectangle A?

( )

Ⓒ How many meters is the length of rectangle A?

( )

98

2 The diagrams below show two fields. In both fields, you will make some paths that have a width of 6 m. If you make paths as shown in diagrams Ⓐ and Ⓑ below, how many m² is the area of each of the fields' shaded green areas?   (20 points each)

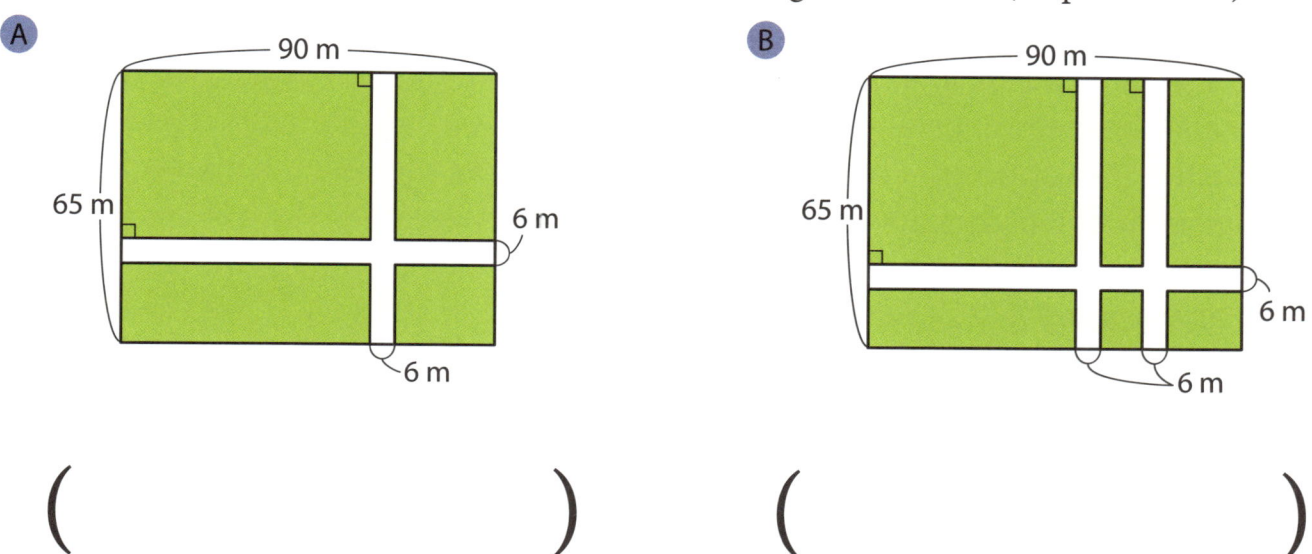

Ⓐ

90 m

65 m

6 m

6 m

Ⓑ

90 m

65 m

6 m

6 m

(   ) (   )

It is helpful to imagine moving the paths and collecting them at the edge of each shape before calculating the area of each remaining shaded space.

Areas of parallelograms

The shapes of parallelograms are different from rectangles and squares, but you can find the areas of parallelograms even though you have not learned how to do this. The opposite sides of parallelograms are parallel and the distance between the two sides are equal in all places. When one of the sides is set as a "base," then the distance between the two opposite sides is the "height" of the parallelogram.

If you cut part of a parallelogram (the shaded triangle, as shown in the diagram on the right) and move it to the opposite side, you can make a rectangle that has the same area as the original parallelogram.

So, you can find the area of the parallelogram by using this formula: Area of a parallelogram = Base × Height

The key idea here is to think about changing the shape of a parallelogram to a rectangle while keeping the area the same. This works because we already know how to find the area of rectangles.

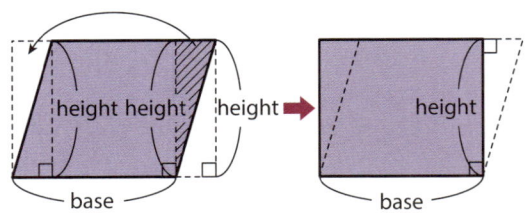

Z-kai
Zoom-Up Workbook
Math
Answers & Solutions

Grade
3

How to use the Answers and Solutions Section

Point 1:

Answers lists correct answers to all problems.

Point 2:

How to Think and Solve discusses thinking and solution processes.

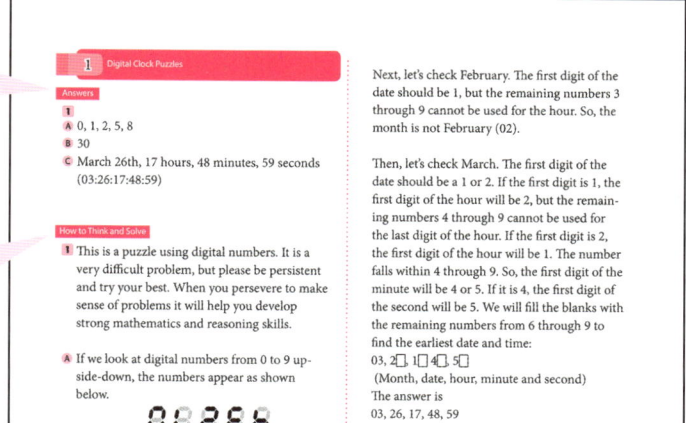

Problems in the Zoom-Up Workbook are not limited to the typical grade level content you learn in most math classes; however, many problems are solvable using mathematics knowledge and skills you have learned so far, if you know how to apply what you know. Most Zoom-Up problems are challenging, but the problems will help you develop problem solving skills, logical reasoning skills, explanation skills and perseverance.

When you solve these problems successfully, your confidence for learning mathematics will increase and you will become a great problem solver and a good young mathematician!

❶ Please check your answers carefully and think about the solutions discussed in the "Answers and Solutions" section.

❷ Then score and add up the points according to the points guide given in each problem.

❸ If you make a mistake, read "How to Think and Solve" carefully and reflect on your solution process. Do not erase your mistakes; instead, keep a record of each error. Use a different color pen when you revise the solution and write down a clear explanation of how you made each mistake. What was your thinking and why was it incorrect? What things do you want to be sure to remember the next time? You will learn so much more if you think carefully and take your time to record what you have learned!

■ Dear Parents, Dear Teachers,

This "Answers and Solutions" section of the Zoom-Up Workbook explains answers and gives helpful points for thinking about and solving each problem. Detailed solution processes are included for most of the challenging problems. Although the Zoom-Up Workbook is designed for students to study challenging problems on their own, it is helpful if parents and teachers read this book and support a student's learning by discussing the details. It may be helpful to provide clues that will help students understand solution processes. The book contains very challenging problems, so it is important for parents and teachers to help encourage students' interest in solving problems and to enjoy the challenge.

Answers

1

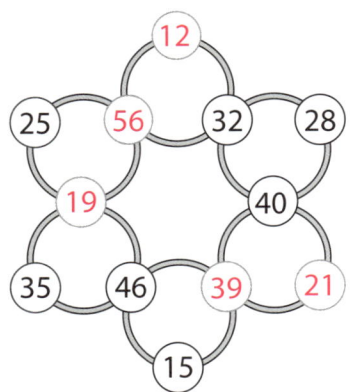

2

6	11	10
13	9	5
8	7	12

3

14	7	12	1
11	2	13	8
5	16	3	10
4	9	6	15

How to Think and Solve

1 First, find the sum of the 3 numbers of the ring with 32, 28, and 40 (on the top right side): 32 + 28 + 40 = 100. Now that you know the sum, look for the rings that have only one missing number. Soon you will easily find the missing numbers for all the remaining rings.

2 The sum of the three numbers in the middle row is 13 + 9 + 5 = 27. Now you know the sum for each column, row, and diagonal. Next, you can look for the columns that have two known numbers and one missing number. Continue to look for places that have only one missing number. Fill the boxes appropriately.

3 The sum of the four numbers in one of the columns is 7 + 2 + 16 + 9 = 34. Now that you know the sum, you can fill the rows that have three known numbers and one missing number. Then study the remaining empty boxes and fill them appropriately.

Answers

1

Ⓐ 7,002　Ⓑ 5,050　Ⓒ 80

2

Ⓐ 9,628　Ⓑ 4,070

3 5,079

4

Ⓐ 8,800, 9,400, 9,800

Ⓑ

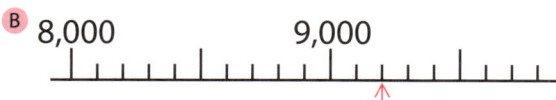

Ⓒ 9,100

Ⓓ 400

5

Ⓐ 7,000　Ⓑ 9,700; 10,000

Ⓒ 5,996　Ⓓ 2,985

How to Think and Solve

3 When you make the smallest number, you need to put the lowest number in the highest place, then put the second lowest number in the second highest place and continue until all place values are filled. It is important to keep in mind that you cannot put 0 in the highest place.

4 For problems Ⓒ and Ⓓ, please use the number line to think about each problem. For problem Ⓓ, consider counting up to the right by 100s from 8,800 to 9,200 and keep track by saying "100, 200, 300, ...".

5 When the missing number ☐ is placed near the beginning of a number sequence it may be difficult to identify the number pattern at first. If so, first look at the numbers to the right of the unknown number to figure out the pattern.

Answers

1

Ⓐ <   Ⓑ >   Ⓒ >

2

Ⓐ 5,630   Ⓑ 8,000   Ⓒ 10,000   Ⓓ 10
Ⓔ 1,400   Ⓕ 900   Ⓖ 2,300   Ⓗ 3,000
Ⓘ 5,000   Ⓙ 100

3

Ⓐ 2,760   Ⓑ 9,959   Ⓒ 5,583   Ⓓ 4,780

4

Ⓐ 1,000   Ⓑ 10,000   Ⓒ 2,400

How to Think and Solve

1 Compare the numbers in the highest place value first.

2 You are challenged to do calculations with large numbers. It is important to think about groups of 100 or 1,000 when calculating. If the calculations are difficult, you may want to think about the problem using number discs (or tiles), or a number line.

3 This problem with large numbers requires you to use the standard algorithm (vertical place-value calculation). The thinking process and procedure are the same whether calculating small or larger multi-digit numbers. Keep that in mind and be confident using the standard algorithm you learned in the past.

4 You will apply previously learned knowledge to do calculations with large numbers.

Ⓐ Calculate the numbers in the brackets first.

Ⓑ You might want to think about a better way to do the calculation. Pay attention to the number in the hundreds place and calculate the numbers that make 10 first.

Ⓒ Do the calculation by thinking about groups of 100. For example, 600 is composed of 6 groups of one hundred. There are 24 (6 × 4 = 24) groups of one hundred. So, the answer is 2,400. If you still find this to be difficult, think about the calculation using the 100-discs (or tiles) to represent the numbers you are calculating.

Answers

1

Ⓐ ① 20 ② 20 ③ 20 ④ 5

Ⓑ 100 Ⓒ 600

In this section, you will learn how to make a challenging calculation easier. Not only will you learn to calculate accurately, but Z-kai hopes that you will develop efficient mental math by thinking about better and easier ways to calculate.

It is very important to discover better ways to calculate, so you can calculate accurately and without much effort. This kind of experience helps you to develop your confidence and interest in learning mathematics.

Z-kai created this section to help you experience the joy of finding a better way to do calculations.

1

Ⓐ This problem should help you make sense of a better and more efficient addition strategy. Focus on pairs of numbers that add up to the same sum.

Ⓑ There are 5 pairs of numbers with a sum of 20. The answer can be easily found by multiplying $20 \times 5 = 100$.

To solve 20×5 mentally, think about 10 groups of 2×5.

There is a story about the famous mathematician, Carl Fredrich Gauss. When Gauss was a little boy he found the sum of all the numbers from 1 to 100 quickly in his head. He noticed 50 pairs of numbers that add up to 101, then found the total sum by multiplying $101 \times 50 = 5,050$.

Ⓒ Use what you learned in problems Ⓐ and Ⓑ. You can make 6 pairs of numbers that add up to 100. So, you can do the mental math of $100 \times 6 = 600$.

5 Algorithm Calculations (Addition)

Answers

*Only the answers to the calculations are provided below. The calculation process is not shown here.

1

Ⓐ 932 Ⓑ 412 Ⓒ 461 Ⓓ 1,226
Ⓔ 1,351 Ⓕ 1,000 Ⓖ 6,632 Ⓗ 7,900
Ⓘ 8,045

2

Ⓐ 8,348 Ⓑ 12,622 Ⓒ 10,000

3

Ⓐ $\begin{array}{r} 289 \\ +\ 345 \\ \hline 634 \end{array}$ Ⓑ $\begin{array}{r} 495 \\ +\ 728 \\ \hline 1223 \end{array}$

Ⓒ $\begin{array}{r} 1824 \\ +\ 2456 \\ \hline 4280 \end{array}$ Ⓓ $\begin{array}{r} 3825 \\ +\ 4587 \\ \hline 8412 \end{array}$

How to Think and Solve

1 These are 3-digit or 4-digit addition problems. Please pay attention to regrouping.
For problems Ⓒ and Ⓕ, think about how place values align in the algorithm calculations.

Ⓒ $\begin{array}{r} 388 \\ +\ \ 73 \\ \hline 461 \end{array}$ Ⓕ $\begin{array}{r} 956 \\ +\ \ 44 \\ \hline 1000 \end{array}$

3 Investigate the numbers starting from the ones place to find the missing numbers in the □. You will need to pay close attention to regrouping place values.

6 Algorithm Calculations (Subtraction)

Answers

*Only the answers to the calculations are provided below. The calculation process is not shown here.

1

Ⓐ 340 Ⓑ 318 Ⓒ 276 Ⓓ 5
Ⓔ 466 Ⓕ 575 Ⓖ 5,742 Ⓗ 548
Ⓘ 608

2

Ⓐ 1,787 Ⓑ 5,876 Ⓒ 3,315

3

Ⓐ $\begin{array}{r} 893 \\ -\ 325 \\ \hline 568 \end{array}$ Ⓑ $\begin{array}{r} 475 \\ -\ 289 \\ \hline 186 \end{array}$

Ⓒ $\begin{array}{r} 5628 \\ -\ 2463 \\ \hline 3165 \end{array}$ Ⓓ $\begin{array}{r} 6435 \\ -\ 4667 \\ \hline 1768 \end{array}$

How to Think and Solve

1 These problems involve 3-digit and 4-digit numbers. When doing subtraction calculations, it is helpful to cross out and rewrite numbers in the process of regrouping.

A The difference in the ones place will be 0. Please don't forget to write 0.

B Regrouping occurs in the ones place.

C Regrouping occurs in the tens place.

D Be careful, the answer is not 005.
Problems **E** through **I** involve regrouping in more than two places. Slow down and pay attention to the calculations in each place.

3 Investigate the numbers starting from the ones place to find the missing numbers in the ☐. After filling the ☐ with numbers, be sure to calculate again to check your answer.

Answers

1 7; 1,000; 999; 999

2
A 998   **B** 997   **C** 994

3 3; 1; 2,000; 1,996

4
A 1,994   **B** 996   **C** 997

How to Think and Solve

1 Understand how to decompose (split) the subtrahend to make mental calculations easy. Note: The subtrahend is the number that is subtracted.

2 Calculate by using a mental calculation strategy in the same way as in problem **1**. Even if you did not come up with a better calculation method, as long as the answer is correct you will earn the point. However, be sure to spend time thinking about and understanding an easier way to calculate, so you can apply this strategy in the future.
If you don't understand how to decompose the subtrahend, think about it in this way: if you want to subtract the number in the ones place of 1,005, then how could you decompose 7? You will immediately see that 7 can be decomposed into 5 and 2. Then you can easily subtract 5 from 1,005 to make 1,000.

4 Even if you did not come up with a better calculation method, as long as the answer is correct you can earn the points. If you don't understand the strategy, please review the strategy used in problem **3** until you understand how it works.

These problems are difficult, so if you do solve them correctly, you should be proud of yourself and your mathematical thinking.

A   996 + 998
   $= 1,000 + 1,000 - 4 - 2$
   $= 2,000 - 4 - 2$
   $= 1,994$

B   497 + 499
   $= 500 + 500 - 3 - 1$
   $= 1,000 - 3 - 1$
   $= 996$

C   299 + 698
   $= 300 + 700 - 1 - 2$
   $= 1,000 - 1 - 2$
   $= 997$

Answers

1

A 6	B 40	C 21	D 36
E 10	F 32	G 24	H 18
I 12	J 25	K 27	L 16
M 35	N 24	O 64	P 63
Q 49	R 36	S 48	T 81

2

A 15	B 24	C 21	D 25
E 63			

3

A   3   ⑥   9   ⑫   15   ⑱   21   ㉔   27

B   3   6   ⑨   12   15   ⑱   21   24   ㉗

112

How to Think and Solve

1 These calculation problems are from the multiplication facts of 2 to 9. Make sure that you know all these multiplication facts.

2 Look at the order of numbers carefully. Logically think about the missing numbers. You may solve these problems by thinking about how the numbers increase or decrease in an orderly way.

Ⓐ These numbers are products of the multiplication facts of 3.

Ⓑ These numbers are products of the multiplication facts of 8 in reverse order.

Ⓒ These numbers are products of the multiplication facts of 7.

Ⓓ These numbers are products of the multiplication facts of 5 in reverse order.

Ⓔ These numbers are products of the multiplication facts of 9 in reverse order.

3 This problem involves relationships among the products of the multiplication facts of 3, 6, and 9.

In problem Ⓐ, products of the multiplication facts of 6 occur as every other number (in the sequence of products in the facts of 3) and next one too. In problem Ⓑ, products of the multiplication facts of 9 appear as every third number. (There are two multiples of 3 between each multiple of 9). If you notice these patterns, the math and you are fantastic!

Answers

1

Ⓐ 4	Ⓑ 9	Ⓒ 7	Ⓓ 6
Ⓔ 7	Ⓕ 2	Ⓖ 4	Ⓗ 5
Ⓘ 7			

2

Ⓐ [Example]

$3 \times 8 = 24$ $4 \times 6 = 24$

$6 \times 4 = 24$ $8 \times 3 = 24$

Ⓑ [Example]

$4 \times 9 = 36$ $6 \times 6 = 36$

$9 \times 4 = 36$

3

Ⓐ $4 \times 4 = 16$ Ⓑ $5 \times 5 = 25$

Ⓒ $7 \times 7 = 49$ Ⓓ $9 \times 9 = 81$

113

1 It is much better for you to solve these problems after you have learned your multiplication facts and can recall them easily. These problems and mastery of multiplication facts will help you understand the concept of division.

A Think about the multiplication facts of 5. Recall $5 \times 1 = 5$, $5 \times 2 = 10$, and so on. You will re-member that $5 \times 4 = 20$. So the missing number in the ☐ is 4. Think about problems **B** through **E** in a similar way.

F Think about $1 \times 5 = 5$, $2 \times 5 = 10$, and so on. You could use the multiplication facts of 5 to investigate this problem by changing the order of multiplier and multiplicand. You have learned that changing the order will not change the product. Think about problems **G** to **I** in a similar way.

2 These problems lead to the concept of "factors" that you will learn about in the upper grades. These problems require a higher-level skill, so you should try these problems after you have mastered the multiplication facts. When you solve 1-digit × 2-digit mutiplication, such as $1 \times 24 = 24$ or $2 \times 12 = 24$ for problem **A**; $1 \times 36 = 36$, $2 \times 18 = 36$, or $3 \times 12 = 36$ for prob-lem **B**, your answer will also be correct and you will earn points.

3 Think about $1 \times 1 = 1$, $2 \times 2 = 4$, $3 \times 3 = 9$, and so on to find the correct products.

Answers

1
A 6   B 4, 4   C 2, 2

2
A 2, 2   B 3   C 5   D 9
E 8   F 5   G 6

3
A 16   B 8, 16   C 3   D 3

4
A 2, 8, 72   B 3, 6, 42

How to Think and Solve

2 When a multiplier increases by 1, the product increases by the multiplicand. You can use this property to solve multiplication problems with large numbers (Remember that the order of numbers in the multiplication sentences in this workbook is "multiplicand × multiplier = product.").

The problems **F** and **G** are application problems. When a multiplier decreases by 1, the product will be decreased by the multiplicand.

3 In problems **A** and **B**, you need to know that the calculations in parentheses ( ) should be calculated first even in the case of multiplication. In problems **C** and **D**, you will learn to decompose one of the numbers in multiplication into two numbers to make a three-number multiplication problem. Compare the left and right sides of the equal sign to figure out what part of the expression on the left side is decomposed.

4 Decompose one number in a two-number multiplication problem to create three numbers. This will help you solve multiplication problems with large numbers.

First, figure out which number is decomposed and put the appropriate number in the first ☐.
Next, compare the multiplication of 3 numbers to the original 2 numbers. This will help you find the appropriate number for the second ☐.

For example, in problem **A**, we compare both sides of the equation: $9 \times \boxed{2} \times 4 = 9 \times \square$ to find the answer of 2×4 for the second ☐.
This is a challenging problem. So, if you can solve this problem, you should be proud of yourself and your mathematical reasoning.

Answers

1

A

20	24	28	32

B

	36	
35	42	49

C

6	12	18
	14	

2 Nathan

115

How to Think and Solve

1 Look at the pattern of numbers carefully and find the multiplication facts that produce the pattern of products.

A When you see the products 20 and 28, you recognize these are products of the multiplication facts of 4. If this is difficult, think about how much each product increases.

B When you see the number 49, you recognize it is a product of the multiplication facts of 7.

C Many multiplication facts have 12 as a product, so you must pay attention to the number 14. Since 14 is either 2×7 or 7×2, you need to investigate the multiplication facts of 2 and 7 by considering the relationship of each fact to the location of the number 12.

2 When you think about multiplication problems that are not part of the multiplication facts 1 – 9, consider thinking about calculating in the following ways:

$2 \times 27 = 2 \times 3 \times 9 = 6 \times 9 = 54$

$24 \times 3 = 8 \times 3 \times 3 = 8 \times 9 = 72$

$18 \times 5 = 9 \times 2 \times 5 = 9 \times 10 = 90$

If you had any difficulty solving these problems, please refer to the section No.10.

Answers

1

A 2, 1   **B** 3, 2

2

A 1   **B** 2   **C** 8, 8   **D** 7

E 6

3 10, 3, 52

4

A 5, 90   **B** 10, 48

C [Example] 10, 8, 108

How to Think and Solve

1 In this section, you will learn about the distributive property of multiplication. First, look at the diagrams and understand that a multiplicand or a multiplier can be decomposed to make it easier to calculate multiplication. Please think about the meaning of a multiplication sentence (product, multiplicand, and multiplier), and think about how to calculate and solve the problem.

2 If this problem is difficult, please think about the meaning of the multiplication sentence by using counters or drawing an array diagram with ●.

A Notice that there are "× 7" in both parentheses. So, the number 4 is decomposed into 3 and another number.

C Think about the unknown numbers that equal the multiplier before it was decomposed.

Ⓓ Notice that there are "× 9" in both parentheses. So, the unknown multiplicand was decomposed into 3 and 4.

3 Look at the diagram carefully and think about how the 13 groups were decomposed into two smaller groups of 4.

4 In problem Ⓒ, you need to think about how to decompose 18. You many decompose it into 11 and 7, 12 and 6, etc. You may be able to solve the problem and find the answer using these methods, but you still may need to do calculations that are not basic multiplication facts (2-9). In these cases, you should think about a better way to decompose 18, so the calculation will be easier (using multiplication facts you know very well). You may decompose 18 into 9 and 9, then you can calculate the product using basic multiplication facts. Is there a different or better way to decompose 18?

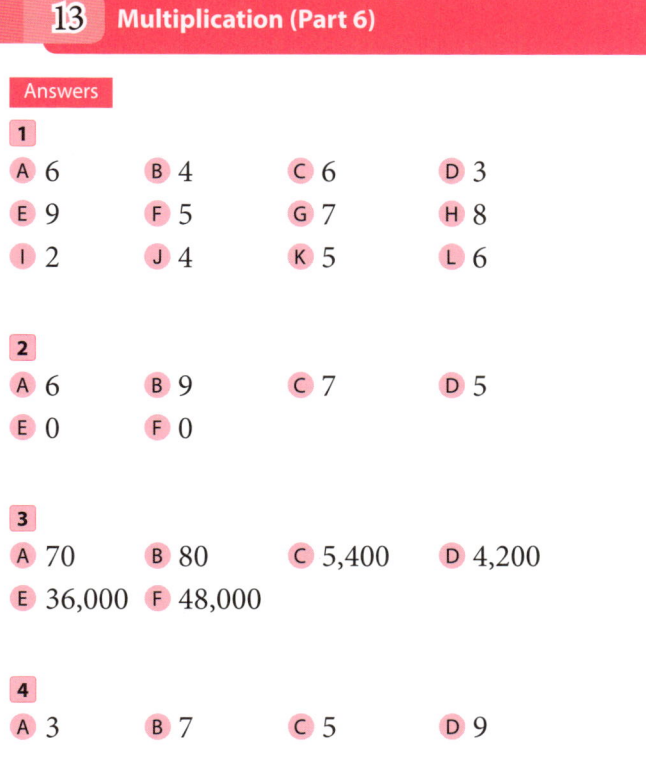

Answers

1

Ⓐ 6	Ⓑ 4	Ⓒ 6	Ⓓ 3
Ⓔ 9	Ⓕ 5	Ⓖ 7	Ⓗ 8
Ⓘ 2	Ⓙ 4	Ⓚ 5	Ⓛ 6

2

| Ⓐ 6 | Ⓑ 9 | Ⓒ 7 | Ⓓ 5 |
| Ⓔ 0 | Ⓕ 0 | | |

3

| Ⓐ 70 | Ⓑ 80 | Ⓒ 5,400 | Ⓓ 4,200 |
| Ⓔ 36,000 | Ⓕ 48,000 | | |

4

| Ⓐ 3 | Ⓑ 7 | Ⓒ 5 | Ⓓ 9 |

How to Think and Solve

1 These multiplication problems are a foundation for understanding division calculations.

Ⓐ Investigate the multiplication facts of 3, 3 × 1 = 3, 3 × 2 = 6, and so on. In the case of 3 × 6 = 18, you are asked to find the appropriate number that completes 3 × ☐ = 18. That missing number is 6. You need to think about a similar way to solve problems Ⓑ through Ⓕ.

Ⓖ Investigate ☐ × 5 = 35 by thinking of 1 × 5 = 5, 2 × 5 = 10, and so on. Even if the order of multiplicand and multiplier is changed, the product stays the same. So, you can use this property and use the multiplication facts of 5 to find the unknown. You need to think in a similar way to solve problems Ⓗ through Ⓛ.

117

2 When solving problems (A) through (C), you need to think about the following property of multiplication: When the multiplier is increased (or decreased) by 1, the product increases (or decreases) by the multiplicand.

(D) For multiplication, even if the order of multiplicand and multiplier is changed, the product stays the same.

(E) and (F)

The product is always 0 when a number is multiplied by 0 (or when 0 is multiplied by a number).

3

(E) There are 36 (4 × 9 = 36) groups of 1,000.

4

(C) The multiplier of 9 could be decomposed to do these calculations, because the product stays the same.

(D) The multiplicand could be decomposed to do the calculation, because the product stays the same.

Answers

1

(A) **Math Sentence:** 4 × 3 = 12
Answer: 12 apples

(B) **Math Sentence:** 3 × 5 = 15
Answer: 15 cucumbers

(C) **Math Sentence:** 5 × 2 = 10
Answer: 10 bananas

2

(A) **Math Sentence:** 2 × 6 = 12
Answer: 12 salmon fillets

(B) **Math Sentence:** 1 × 7 = 7
Answer: 7 lobster tails

How to Think and Solve

The Problem Episodes from No.14 through No.21 are designed to check if you have a basic understanding of multiplication. If you have not learned about multiplication or if you have difficulty understanding multiplication, please try the following for problem **1** (A):

First, think about drawing the problem situation, perhaps using circles to represent the situation with repeated addition (4 + 4 + 4 = 12). Your drawing will help you focus on how many apples are in each basket, how many baskets there are, and how many apples there are altogether. Then you will be ready to establish a multiplication sentence. For example, 4 apples in each basket multiplied by 3 baskets equals 12 apples altogether, so 4 × 3 = 12. You may have been taught to see 3 groups of 4 apples, and to write the math sentence in the following order: 3 × 4 = 12. However, the Zoom-Up Workbook will always show the multiplication sentence as (number of objects) × (number of groups) = (total number of objects).

We recommend that you understand the meaning of each number in a multiplication sentence and are consistent about how you order the numbers when solving multiplication problems. You will also learn that multiplication follows the commutative property: 4×3 and 3×4 both equal 12. Both 4×3 and 3×4 are correct ways to represent the multiplication problems in this Zoom-Up Workbook.

Another way to think about 3 baskets of 4 apples is as follows: To make the baskets, you put an apple in each basket one at a time. The first time you place 3 apples. The second time you place another 3 apples, and the third time another 3 apples. Finally, the fourth time you place another 3 apples. So, you distributed 3 apples each time and did the process 4 times. That used 12 apples altogether. So, 3 baskets of 4 apples from the original explanation, and this new way of distributing apples both end up with the same total number of apples (12 apples altogether).

Answers

1

Ⓐ **Math Sentence:** $5 \times 7 = 35$
Answer: 35 chicken nuggets

Ⓑ **Math Sentence:** $3 \times 4 = 12$
Answer: 12 spring rolls

Ⓒ **Math Sentence:** $4 \times 6 = 24$
Answer: 24 tacos

2

Ⓐ **Math Sentence:** $1 \times 9 = 9$
Answer: 9 pieces of mochi ice cram

Ⓑ **Math Sentence:** $2 \times 8 = 16$
Answer: 16 pieces of mochi ice cream

How to Think and Solve

The Problem Episodes No.14 and No.15 deal with the multiplication facts of 1 through 5. You may have difficulty understanding the multiplication facts of 1. For example, when you have only 1 apple in each basket and there are 3 baskets, you can count the total number of apples easily without multiplying. It also seems odd to see the situation as 3 groups of 1 apple, since we really do not see 1 apple in a basket as 1 "group" of 1 apple. If you have difficulty seeing this as $1 \times 3 = 3$, then consider comparing this situation with situations for the multiplication facts of 2. Think about 2 apples in each basket and 3 baskets. How many apples are there? You would write $2 \times 3 = 6$, because $2 \times 3 = 6$ shows 2 in each group and there are 3 groups. So, $1 \times 3 = 3$ shows 1 in each group and there are 3 groups.

In supermarkets, you see many things that are packed into packages, boxes, or baskets. So, you can think of many interesting multiplication stories. When you go to the store with your family, surprise them by creating many different multiplication stories!

Answers

1

(A) **Math Sentence:** $9 \times 4 = 36$
Answer: 36 cookies

(B) **Math Sentence:** $8 \times 9 = 72$
Answer: 72 pieces of rice krispies

(C) **Math Sentence:** $6 \times 4 = 24$
Answer: 24 packs

(D) **Math Sentence:** $9 \times 7 = 63$
Answer: 63 pieces of chocolate

(E) **Math Sentence:** $7 \times 3 = 21$
Answer: 21 sticks of gum

How to Think and Solve

This and the next episodes deal with the multiplication facts of 6 through 9. Because there are more items in a group, it may be more difficult to draw each multiplication situation. So, think about the way you represent these multiplication sentences in the same way as you thought about the multiplication facts of 1 through 5.

Create more multiplication stories with your friends. Be sure you write the math sentence and find the answers without rushing. You can find many multiplication situations not only at the supermarket, but in other places or activities in your daily life!

Answers

1

(A) **Math Sentence:** $8 \times 2 = 16$
Answer: 16 slices

(B) **Math Sentence:** $6 \times 5 = 30$
Answer: 30 rolls

(C) **Math Sentence:** $8 \times 6 = 48$
Answer: 48 slices

(D) **Math Sentence:** $9 \times 2 = 18$
Answer: 18 pieces of fried chicken

(E) **Math Sentence:** $7 \times 4 = 28$
Answer: 28 pieces of sushi

How to Think and Solve

This problem episode involves multiplication from 6 through 9. You may be able to solve these problems easily, but you may also find a few of the problems to be difficult. This is one reason why it is good to know about the properties of multiplication.

For example, even when you switch the order of two factors (numbers), the answer is the same: 3×2 is as same as 2×3 and $5 \times 7 = 7 \times 5$. So, even when you see 7×5 as a multiplication fact of 7, you can use 5×7 from the multiplication facts of 5 to find the answer.

The products (answers) of the multiplication facts of 9 show a very interesting pattern. For example, the products of the facts of 9 are 9, 18, 27, 36, 45, 54, 63, 72, 81. The sum of the numbers in the ones and the tens place in each of these products equals 9!

The numbers 21, 42, and 63 each have a number in the tens place that is 2 times as much as the number in the ones place. Do you notice that 21, 42, and 63 are all products of multiplication of 7? The numbers 147, 168, and 189 are also multiples of 7! Please check to make sure if that is true. Learning math with such interesting discoveries as these is what makes math fun!

1

Ⓐ **Math Sentence:** $7 \times 2 = 14$
Answer: 14 sticks

Ⓑ **Math Sentence:** $7 \times 0 = 0$
Answer: 0 sticks

2

Ⓐ **Math Sentence:** $2 \times 4 = 8$
Answer: 8 points

Ⓑ **Math Sentence:** $0 \times 3 = 0$
Answer: 0 points

How to Think and Solve

The theme of this episode is multiplication of zero (0). You may have some difficulty understanding the concept of multiplication of zero. Memorizing the method is not enough. It is good to compare multiplication with 0 to other multiplication facts.

1 This problem aims to develop understanding of the calculation 7×0 by comparing it with 7×2. You may have difficulty understanding multiplication of 0. Please think about "When there are 2 packs of 7 sticks of gum, there are $7 \times 2 = 14$ sticks. When there is one pack of 7 sticks of gum, there are $7 \times 1 = 7$ sticks. Then, when there are 0 packs of 7 sticks of gum (when you buy no gum at all), how many sticks? If you are still puzzled about multiplying 0 packs, you might want to create diagrams similar to the following.

2 packages	▦ ▦	$7 \times 2 = 14$
1 packages	▦	$7 \times 1 = 7$
0 packages		$7 \times 0 = 0$

-7
-7

When the number of packs decreases by 1, the number of sticks of gum decreases by 7. So, if you consider this pattern you can establish the multiplication sentence 7×0 and find the answer is 0.

2 It is relatively easy to explain how to calculate 0×3. If you have difficulty understanding, try making cards. Each card represents a stick of gum that is worth some points. Then think about how you would explain this problem. When there are 4 sticks of gum and each is worth 2 points, you could find the total number of points by adding $2 + 2 + 2 + 2 = 8$. That can also be written as multiplication, $2 \times 4 = 8$. In the same way, when there are 3 sticks of gum and each is worth 0 points, you could find the total points by adding $0 + 0 + 0 = 0$. That can be written as multiplication also, $0 \times 3 = 0$.

1

Ⓐ **Math Sentence:** $6 \times 9 = 54$
 Answer: 54 stars
Ⓑ **Math Sentence:** $54 + 6 = 60$
 Answer: 60 stars
Ⓒ **Math Sentence:** $60 + 6 = 66$
 Answer: 66 stars

2

Ⓐ **Math Sentence:** $6 \times 10 = 60$
 Answer: 60 stars
Ⓑ **Math Sentence:** $6 \times 11 = 66$
 Answer: 66 stars

The theme of this episode is about multiplication with numbers greater than 10. Although these calculations are not included in regular multiplication facts to 10, you can solve these problems by thinking about a property of multiplication.

As the number of groups increases by 1, the total increases by the number of objects in each group. For example, let's look at the multiplication facts of 6: when the number of groups increases by 1, the product (total) increases by 6. If you know $6 \times 9 = 54$, then you can find 6×10 by adding 6 to 54, because the number of groups increased by 1 (from 9 to 10). So, the product of $6 \times 10 = 60$. Now consider that 6×11 has 1 more group than 6×10, so you can add 6 to 60 to make 66.

You can also think about 6×11 by starting from 6×9. What can you do? Since the number of groups increases by 2, the product increases by $6 + 6 = 12$. So, the product of $6 \times 11 = 66$. You may also want to use counters to investigate the relationships among multiplication facts. This can often help you see the relationships clearly.

Since multiplication follows the commutative property, you could think of 6×10 (6 multiplied by 10) as 10×6 (10 multiplied by 6) to find the answer (product). 10×6 shows there are 6 groups of 10, and it is easier to find the answer to 6×10 than thinking about 10 groups of 6.

Answers

1

A **Math Sentence:** $5 \times 4 = 20$
Answer: 20 cards

B **Math Sentence:** $8 \times 4 = 32$ or
$(5 \times 4) + (3 \times 4) = 20 + 12 = 32$
Answer: 32 cards
You could write the math sentence as
$(5 + 3) \times 4 = 8 \times 4 = 32$

2

A **Math Sentence:** $3 \times 4 = 12$ $(4 \times 3 = 12)$
Answer: 12 cards

B **Math Sentence:** $3 \times 2 = 6$
Answer: 6 cards

C **Math Sentence:** $13 \times 4 = 52$
Answer: 52 cards

How to Think and Solve

The goal of this episode is for you to understand the distributive property of multiplication.

1

B 5 cards are distributed to each player first, then 3 more cards are distributed to each player. So, the total number of cards distributed to each person is 8 cards. You can write the math sentence in this way: $(5 + 3) \times 4 = 8 \times 4 = 32$

Another method is to find the total number of cards distributed the first time, then find the total number of cards distributed the second time. Finally, add these two products together. You can write the math sentence in this way: $(5 \times 4) + (3 \times 4) = 20 + 12 = 32$

Because the first and the second methods produce the same result (32 cards), you can represent this relationship as: $(5 + 3) \times 4 = (5 \times 4) + (3 \times 4)$

This relationship is called the "distributive property of multiplication."

2

B Hearts and Diamonds are red suit cards. Each suit has 3 face cards.

C The distributive property of multiplication is very useful when you think about this problem. There are 4 different suits and each suit has 13 cards, so we can find the total number of cards as 13×4. If you think about 13 as 10 and 3, then you can think about 13×4 as $(10 + 3) \times 4 = (10 \times 4) + (3 \times 4) = 40 + 12 = 52$.

The distributive property is also useful for calculating numbers greater than 10, such as 13×12.
$13 \times 12 = 13 \times (10 + 2) = (13 \times 10) + (13 \times 2) = 130 + 26 = 156$
Of course you need to know how to calculate 13×10 and 13×2. However, you can use the distributive property to make these calculations easier too, such as $13 \times 2 = (10 \times 2) + (3 \times 2) = 20 + 6 = 26$. Now you can see how useful the distributive property can be. It certainly makes calculations easier.

Answers

1

Calculation	Score
7 × 4 = 28	28 points
9 × 5 = 45	45 points
10 × 6 = 60	60 points
13 × 3 = 39	39 points

2

Ⓐ 1st game

Calculation	Score
7 × 3 = 21	21 points
10 × 5 = 50	50 points

2nd game

Calculation	Score
9 × 6 = 54	54 points
6 × 4 = 24	24 points

Ⓑ **Math Sentence:** 50 + 24 = 74
Answer: 74 points

Ⓒ **Math Sentence:** 116 – 74 = 42
Answer: 42 points

Ⓓ **Number:** 7
Suit: ♦

How to Think and Solve

This is a problem that involves multiplication. Be sure to understand the card game's rules, analyze the table carefully, and calculate the scores correctly.

2

Ⓓ Among the multiplication facts, only 6 × 7 and 7 × 6 have a product of 42. According to the rule, the multiplier is either 3, 4, 5 or 6. From this, we can identify the number on the card as 7 and the suit as ♥.

Answers

1

Ⓐ 7	Ⓑ 3	Ⓒ 2	Ⓓ 4
Ⓔ 7	Ⓕ 6	Ⓖ 6	Ⓗ 3
Ⓘ 7	Ⓙ 1	Ⓚ 0	Ⓛ 0

2

Ⓐ 14	Ⓑ 0	Ⓒ 1	Ⓓ 36

3 B, E

4 [Example 1]

There are 30 oranges. If we give 5 oranges to each friend, how many friends will get 5 oranges?

[Example 2]

There are 30 students. If we make 5 teams with an equal number of students, how many students will be on each team?

---

1 For problems Ⓐ through Ⓙ, you need to think about using the multiplication facts of the divisors. For problems Ⓚ and Ⓛ, you need to think about the appropriate numbers that fill each box, such as $6 \times \square = 0$ and $8 \times \square = 0$.
Because
$$0 \div 6 = \square \rightarrow 6 \times \square = 0$$
$$0 \div 8 = \square \rightarrow 8 \times \square = 0$$

2 For problems Ⓐ and Ⓓ, think about this: When a dividend is divided by 1, the answer is always the same as the dividend.

Ⓑ When 0 is divided by a number that is not 0, the answer is always 0.

Ⓒ When a dividend and a divisor are the same number (but not 0), the answer is always 1.

3 The word problems B and E represent division, $9 \div 3$. Problems A and C represent multiplication and problem D represents subtraction.

4 This problem is asking you to make a division word problem that represents $30 \div 5$. Creating problems helps you develop the ability to interpret a math sentence by thinking of concrete problem situations which represent $30 \div 5$. If you have difficulty creating problem situations, then think of similar word problem situations. In the answer section above for this problem, examples [1] and [2] are given to help you. When you learn to think of several different problem situations that represent a math sentence, then the math and you are awesome!

Answers

1

Ⓐ 10　　Ⓑ 10　　Ⓒ 15　　Ⓓ 13

Ⓔ 12　　Ⓕ 12

2

Ⓐ 50　　Ⓑ 100　　Ⓒ 200　　Ⓓ 300

3

Ⓐ ① 14　② 28　③ 42　④ 56　⑤ 4

Ⓑ 5　　Ⓒ 4

How to Think and Solve

1 This problem involves division problems that are not answered simply by using multiplication facts one time.

Ⓐ 30 has 3 groups of 10, so 3 ÷ 3 = 1

Each group contains 10, so 30 ÷ 3 = 10

Ⓑ Think in the same way as Ⓐ.

Ⓒ Decompose 45 into 30 and 15.

30 ÷ 3 = 10

15 ÷ 3 = 5

The sum of the answers is 15.

So, 45 ÷ 3 = 15

Ⓓ to Ⓕ

Think about these calculations by decomposing 52 into 40 and 12, 72 into 60 and 12, and 96 into 80 and 16.

2 These divisions involve dividends that are multiples of a hundred.

Ⓐ 200 has 20 groups of 10 (20 tens), so 20 ÷ 4 = 5.

Each group contains 10 and there are 5 groups of 10.

So, the answer is 50.

Ⓑ 500 has 5 groups of 100 (5 hundreds),

so 5 ÷ 5 = 1

Each group contains 100, so the answer is 100.

Ⓒ and Ⓓ

Think about these calculations in the same way as you did for problem Ⓐ.

3

Ⓑ and Ⓒ

Think about using multiplication sentences and ☐ for the missing number (multiple).

Answers

1

Ⓐ **Math Sentence:** $32 \div 4 = 8$

Answer: 8 students

Ⓑ **Math Sentence:** $800 \div 4 = 200$

Answer: 200 counters

2

Ⓐ **Math Sentence:** $6 \times 6 = 36, 36 \div 4 = 9$

Answer: 9 counters

Ⓑ **Math Sentence:** $36 \div 3 = 12$

Answer: 12 counters

How to Think and Solve

1 You need to split the counters into equal groups; then problems Ⓐ and Ⓑ can be solved by division.

In problem Ⓑ, think of 800 split into groups of 100 (or 8 hunreds). When you solve the division $800 \div 4$, you could think it as 8 groups of $100 \div 4 = 2$ groups of 100 (or 8 hundreds $\div 4 = 2$ hundreds). So, the answer is 200.

2 This problem uses both multiplication and division. The problem asks you to rearrange counters so the square is changed to a rectangle. Keep the same number of counters.

Ⓐ First, find the number of counters. There are 6 counters to a side of the rectangle. So, there are 6 rows of 6 counters in each row. The total number of counters is $6 \times 6 = 36$.

Second, the problem asks you to change the height of the square. You can do this if you change the height to 4 counters. Then, when you divide 36 by 4, the number in the bottom row will be $36 \div 4 = 9$ counters.

Ⓑ When you answer a division problem that is not your basic single-digit multiplication fact, then there is a way to make it easier to solve. You can split the dividend (total number) into "friendly" numbers that are easier to divide by 3.

In this problem, you can split the dividend 36 into 30 and 6. (30 is a friendly number that can be divided by 3.)

So,

$$30 \div 3 = 10$$
$$6 \div 3 = 2$$

The sum is 12

128

Answers

1

Ⓐ **Math Sentence:** $52 \div 6 = 8$ Remainder 4

$8 + 1 = 9$

Answer: 9 tents

Ⓑ ① 5 ② 20 ③ 25 ④ 10
⑤ 17 ⑥ 27 ⑦ 15 ⑧ 37
⑨ 52

Ⓒ B. 10 people   C. 20 people
D. 17 people

How to Think and Solve

1

Ⓐ Until now, you may not have learned about division problems with "remainders," but Z-kai includes these problems to develop your problem solving skills. When you solve unfamiliar problems, you need to recall what you have learned before, then think about how to use that knowledge to solve the new problems.

You did not have to use division to solve this problem. Instead, you could have used multiplication, as follows:

Think about the multiplication facts of 6 and how many tents it would take for all 52 people to sleep in a tent.

When there are 8 tents, $6 \times 8 = 48$ (people can sleep in tents).

When there are 9 tents, $6 \times 9 = 54$ (people can sleep in tents).

52 people came to the camp. If they have 8 tents $52 - 48 = 4$ (people) will not fit in the tents. They will be left outside! Since these 4 people must also sleep in a tent, you will need to add 1 more tent. Therefore, you need a total of $8 + 1 = 9$ tents in order for all campers to sleep in tents.

Ⓑ This problem challenges you to think logically about different conditions of groups of people.

From the information given in the problem, you can start filling numbers in the following order of ⑦, ③, and ①. ⑦ is 15, ③ is 25, and ① is 5.
② can be found by $25 - 5 = 20$.
④ can be found by $15 - 5 = 10$.
⑤ can be found by $5 + 20 + 10 = 35$ and $52 - 35 = 17$.
⑥ can be found by $10 + 17 = 27$.
⑧ can be found by $20 + 17 = 37$.
If your calculation of ③ + ⑥ = 52 and ⑦ + ⑧ = 52 are correct, you can avoid calculation mistakes.

Ⓒ This problem challenges you to think logically about the relationship of different conditions of groups in the Venn Diagram. Even if you have never learned how to create or read a Venn Diagram, you can figure it out by carefully thinking about the description of the problem. The key to solving this problem is understanding what each area of the diagram is representing logically.

Area B represents the people who caught only trout.

Area C represents the people who caught only catfish.

Area D represents the people who did not catch either trout or catfish.

Answers

1

Ⓐ **Math Sentence:** 45 – 20 = 25

Answer: 25

Ⓑ 7 times

Ⓒ **Math Sentence:** 45 + 5 + 20 + 35 = 105

6 × 105 = 630

Answer: 630 legs

2 **Math Sentence:** 2 kg = 2,000 g

600 g + 300 g = 900 g

2,000 g – (600 g + 900 g) = 500 g

Answer: 500 g

How to Think and Solve

1

Ⓐ When you read a bar graph, it is important to understand how much is represented by one increment of a tick mark on the graph. There are 2 increments (2 tick marks) from 0 to 10. So, each increment represents 5 insects.

Ⓑ By comparing the number of increments, you can find the answer easily. The bar that represents ladybugs in the graph is 7 increments high. The bar that represents dragonflies is only 1 increment. So, the number of ladybugs is 7 times as many as the number of dragonflies. If you can read the graph, you can find the actual number of ladybugs. Each increment represents 5 in the graph. The bar for ladybugs is 7 increments high, so the number of ladybugs was 5 × 7 = 35. The bar for dragonflies is only 1 increment, so the number of dragonflies was 1 × 5 = 5.

You can use division to find how many times as many ladybugs there were as the number of dragonflies.

35 ÷ 5 = 7 (times)

Ⓒ There are two methods to find the total number of insects: (1) find the number of each kind of insect, then add them all together, or (2) find the total number of increments in the bars of the graph, then multiply the increments by 5.

The first method: 45 + 5 + 20 + 35 = 105

The second method: (9 + 1 + 4 + 7) × 5 = 21 × 5 = (20 + 1) × 5 = (20 × 5) + (1 × 5) = 100 + 5 = 105.

Finally, all insects have 6 legs, so the total number of legs on 105 insects can be found by 105 × 6 = (100 + 5) × 6 = (100 × 6) + (5 × 6)= 600 + 30 = 630 (legs).

2 1 kg = 1,000 g. So, the weight of the 2 kg watermelon is 2,000 g.

600 g is how much Nashita ate.

600 g + 300 g = 900 g is how much Chang ate.

The problem is asking how many grams of watermelon is left, so 2,000 – (600 + 900) = 500 (g)

The "k" in "kg" and in "km" means 1,000 times greater. So, 1 kg means 1,000 times greater than 1 g (1,000 g = 1 kg), and 1km means 1,000 times greater than 1 m (1,000 m = 1 km).

1

Ⓐ **Math Sentence:** $3 \times 3 = 9$, $9 \times 8 = 72$
Answer: 72 counters

Ⓑ **Math Sentence:** $9 \times 9 = 81$, $3 \times 3 = 9$
$\qquad\qquad\quad 81 - 9 = 72$
Answer: 72 counters

Ⓒ **Math Sentence:** $6 \times 3 = 18$, $18 \times 4 = 72$
Answer: 72 counters

1 Up till now, you may not have had many experiences exploring and discussing different ways to solve a math problem. This problem gives you the experience of thinking about many different solutions.

It is important for elementary students to explore and discuss many different ways to solve a problem. Through these experiences, Z-kai believes that students will learn to look more closely and examine problems to find an efficient way to solve them. This can be accomplished by comparing, noticing, and understanding "outside-the-box" ideas that will become effective ways to solve problems. When you discuss similar solutions with your friends, you will see how you can generalize important ideas.

You should be proud of yourself if you learn how to find many different solution methods. You should be happy to learn new strategies by exchanging ideas with your classmates through discussion. If you begin to feel that learning different strategies is interesting, your mathematical thinking, knowledge, and skills will also improve.

Ⓒ 18×4 can be calculated by splitting 18 into 10 and 8.
$10 \times 4 = 40$, $8 \times 4 = 32$
So, $40 + 32 = 72$
This calculation idea uses the distributive property.
$18 \times 4 = (10 + 8) \times 4 = (10 \times 4) + (8 \times 4) = 40 + 32 = 72$

Answers

1

Ⓐ 7

Ⓑ **Math Sentence:** $56 \div 7 = 8$
Answer: 8 m

2

Ⓐ 800　　Ⓑ 800　　Ⓒ 10　　Ⓓ 80

Ⓔ 1　　Ⓕ 81

How to Think and Solve

Problem Episodes No.28 and No.29 are division application problems. These are classic problems and are given a special name in Japan. They are called "Ueki-zan." The word "ueki" means "plants" and "zan" means "calculation." These problems may be challenging for you if you usually draw a picture to think about a problem. So, a diagram is included for you to use to think about the problem.

1 Please read the dialogue carefully and study the problem situation until you understand the "Ueki-zan" method. Because we are trying to find the distance between trees, you should not divide the total length by the number of trees. Because the number of spaces between trees is not given in the problem, this problem is particularly challenging, especially representing it in a math sentence.

2 The key point you need to understand is that the number of seeds is 1 greater than the number of spaces between the seeds. In problem **1**, the number of trees is 8 and the number of spaces between trees is 7. This can be a hint to help you think about problem **2**. Remember solution methods that you learned previously and utilize them to solve new problems. Seeing connections to what you learned before will help you improve your thinking and problem-solving skills. This problem episode also involves converting length units (changing one unit into a different unit of length). When the units are different, it is important to think about how you can convert a unit to make calculation easier.

Answers

1

Ⓐ **Math Sentence:** $48 \div 4 = 12$

  Answer: 12 spaces

Ⓑ 12 flowers

Ⓒ **Math Sentence:** $48 \div 8 = 6$

  Answer: 6 m

How to Think and Solve

In this problem, you are asked to think about planting, and measuring a distance that is not in a straight line, but in a circle (around a pond). An important goal of the Zoom-Up Workbook is to develop your strong problem-solving skills that will be necessary to solve new and different problem situations.

1

Ⓐ First, find the number of spaces between the flowers. To find the answer use division, $48 \div 4$. Split 48 into 40 and 8 in the same way as in problem **2** Ⓑ of Problem Episode No.24.

Ⓑ A straight line has two end points; however, the pond in this problem is a circle. A circle has no end point. In this case, the number of flowers is the same as the number of spaces. This is a key idea for solving this problem.

If you did not notice the difference between the case of the straight road and the circular pond, then you may have added 1 to your calculation in the same way as in the previous episode. This would give an answer of 13 flowers. Please refer to the diagram in the box "If you can solve this, the math-*and you*-are cool!," then check the number of flowers and spaces again.

Drawing diagrams helps you understand a problem clearly. A diagram also helps to reflect your thinking process and to justify your solution. So, it is a good idea to draw a diagram when you are solving difficult problems.

Ⓒ There are 8 spaces between flowers. In our daily lives, a plan may be changed from its original idea. If you are able to adjust your thinking based on changes to a problem situation, your thinking and problem solving will improve … and become fantastic!

Answers

1

Ⓐ $\dfrac{1}{4}$ Ⓑ $\dfrac{1}{2}$ Ⓒ $\dfrac{1}{8}$

2 4

3

Ⓐ [Example]   Ⓑ [Example]   Ⓒ [Example]

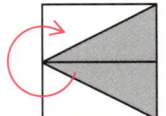

4 2, $\dfrac{1}{4}$

5

Ⓐ $\dfrac{1}{4}$ Ⓑ $\dfrac{1}{2}$ Ⓒ $\dfrac{1}{4}$

How to Think and Solve

3 In problems Ⓐ and Ⓑ, the squares (a whole) are divided into four parts. So, color one of the parts of the square in each problem to represent one-fourth. In problem Ⓒ, the square is divided into 16 parts. Color one-fourth by referring to what was shaded in problem Ⓐ. If four parts are colored in problem Ⓒ, the same area is colored as in problem Ⓐ; therefore, you are correct. Both represent one-fourth.

5 In problems Ⓑ and Ⓒ, you can solve the problems easily. Just move one of the shaded parts as indicated by the arrows below.

Ⓐ

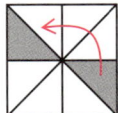

Ⓑ

Answers

1

Ⓐ $\dfrac{1}{7}$ Ⓑ 8   Ⓒ 5

2

Ⓐ $\dfrac{9}{13}$ m   Ⓑ 3 times

3

Ⓐ <   Ⓑ >

4

Ⓐ $\dfrac{5}{8}$ Ⓑ $\dfrac{3}{7}$

5

Ⓐ $\dfrac{1}{8}$ $\dfrac{3}{8}$ $\dfrac{5}{8}$ $\dfrac{6}{8}$

Ⓑ $\dfrac{2}{9}$ $\dfrac{4}{9}$ $\dfrac{5}{9}$ 1

Ⓒ $\dfrac{1}{10}$ $\dfrac{1}{5}$ $\dfrac{1}{4}$ $\dfrac{1}{3}$

How to Think and Solve

1

Ⓐ The fraction $\frac{6}{7}$ is made of six $\frac{1}{7}$ s.

Ⓑ The denominator represents how many parts 1L was divided into.

Ⓒ The numerator represents how many of the 6 equal parts of 1m are being considered.

2 You are comparing the length of 2 tapes. Think about how many parts the 1m is divided into first, then identify how long each length of tape is in fraction form.

3 The problem asks you to compare the sizes of two fractions. When two fractions have the same denominator, the fraction that has the greater numerator is greater than the other fraction and you compare the numerators.

4 You may want to convert 1 into a fraction and/or use a number line to think about this problem.

5 You need to compare the sizes of four fractions. When fractions have the same denominator, the fraction that has a greater numerator will be greater. When fractions have the same numerator, the fraction that has a smaller denominator is greater.

Answers

1

Ⓐ 1 hour 20 minutes

Ⓑ 50 minutes

Ⓒ Tomy ran 30 minutes more than Robert.

Ⓓ 10:10

Ⓔ 11:10

Ⓕ 9:16

135

How to Think and Solve

The theme of this problem episode is time. Based on the understanding that 1 hour is equal to 60 minutes, you will learn about the addition and subtraction of time periods, which we call "elapsed time." Elapsed time is the length of time that occurs between a starting and an ending point in time.

1

Ⓐ From your calculations, you find that Robert ran 80 minutes. Since the problem is asking "How many hours and minutes did he run?," you have to convert 80 minutes to an hour and some minutes. Since 60 minutes = 1 hour, subtract 60 minutes from 80 minutes to find how many minutes are left after 1 hour (60 minutes): 80 − 60 = 20 (minutes)

For problems Ⓑ and Ⓒ, you may find it easier to convert the time into minutes first before solving the problems.

For problems Ⓓ and Ⓔ, you need to understand how time passes and the order or position of the runners. This will help you to think about whether you need to use addition or subtraction.

In problems Ⓐ through Ⓔ you learned to calculate time and elapsed time (a given time period) by thinking about 10-minute increments. In problem Ⓕ, you will calculate time in 1-minute increments. There are two ways to solve this problem: (1) convert 76 minutes into 1 hour 16 minutes, or (2) split 20 minutes into 4 minutes and 16 minutes.

Answers

1

Ⓐ 10:50

Ⓑ 1:10

Ⓒ 5 hours 30 minutes

Ⓓ 3:00 p.m.

Ⓔ Tomy, the turtle, arrived 10 minutes before Robert, the rabbit.

How to Think and Solve

Problem Episodes No.32 and No.33 are focused on the calculation of elapsed time, and expressing times using "a.m." or "p.m.."

1

Ⓐ In this problem, you need to find the time that is 80 minutes after 9:30. If you convert 80 minutes into an hour and minutes, it is easy to calculate the time. Or you could solve this problem by finding the time to 10:00 first, then subtracting those minutes from 80 minutes. You may want to look at both these solution methods and think about the merits of using the different methods.

Ⓑ Make sure you understand that the time 2:20 is 80 minutes after 1:00. You may want to split 70 minutes into 20 minutes and 50 minutes, then think about the time as 50 minutes before 2:00.

Ⓒ In this problem, the time period runs from a.m. to p.m. You could find the time periods from 7:30 a.m. to 12:00 p.m. and from 12:00 p.m. to 1:00 p.m., then add these two elapsed times to find the total time period (from 7:30 a.m. to 1:00 p.m.). You could also convert 1:00 p.m. to 13:00 and find the difference between 7:30 and 13:00.

D This problem also involves time periods that start in the a.m. and end in the p.m.. However, this problem is different from problem C. This problem doesn't require you to find the difference between starting and ending times. Instead, you are identifying the clock's time after a period of time has passed from a given time (4 hours after 11:00 a.m.).

E Solve the problem using the result of problem D. It is a good idea to draw a diagram or create a timeline to keep track of the time that Robert and Tomy both took to reach Wonderland Park.

34 Time and Elapsed Time

Answers

1

A 180   B 1, 25   C 70   D 5, 5

E 220

2 D → F → A → B → E → C

3

A

	1 hour 50 minutes
+	4 hours 20 minutes
	6 hours 10 minutes

B

	24 minutes 25 seconds
−	17 minutes 38 seconds
	6 minutes 47 seconds

C

	1 day 6 hours 32 minutes 14 seconds
+	10 hours 36 minutes 45 seconds
	1 day 17 hours 8 minutes 59 seconds

4 Naomi solved the problems 5 seconds faster than Teddy.

How to Think and Solve

1 You need to know 1 minute = 60 seconds to solve these problems.

2 Convert the times into minutes from A to F to compare easily.

3 This problem involves algorithm calculations using various units of time.
Be careful about regrouping calculations. Time units change every 60 units, from second to minute and from minute to hour.

A Regroup minutes up to the hour unit.

B Regroup down from the minutes unit to add 60 to 25 seconds.

C Regroup minutes up to the hour unit.

4 Convert the time that Naomi took to solve the problems (1 minute 8 seconds) into seconds (68 seconds). Then, compare 68 seconds to Teddy's time, 73 seconds.

Answers

1

A 2 hours 15 minutes

B **Math Sentence:** 368 + 409 = 777
Answer: 777 students

C **Math Sentence:** 409 − 368 = 41
Answer: 41 boys

2

A **Math Sentence:** $10 \times 0 = 0$, $8 \times 9 = 72$,
$5 \times 7 = 35$, $2 \times 1 = 2$,
$0 \times 3 = 0$,
$0 + 72 + 35 + 2 + 0 = 109$

Answer: 109 points

B Benjamin

How to Think and Solve

1

Ⓐ To think about how much time will pass before the assembly, it is good idea to think about a number related to the nearest hour. For example, 6:45 a.m. is 15 minutes away from 7:00 a.m. Then 7:00 a.m. to 9:00 a.m. is 2 more hours. So, the total duration (elapsed time) is 2 hours and 15 minutes.

Ⓑ Please be careful about the calculation in the tens place because it involves regrouping.

Ⓒ To calculate the tens place, you need to regroup 1 from the hundreds place: $10 - 6 = 4$.

2 In this problem, you are applying multiplication to a school situation. The problem checks your understanding of multiplication with 10 and 0, as well as your ability to extract and use important data from the table.

Ⓐ You should understand that "0 multiplied by any number is 0" and "Any number multiplied by 0 is 0."

Ⓑ The calculations below show how Greg got 106 points.

$10 \times 3 = 30$ $8 \times 2 = 16$
$5 \times 10 = 50$ $2 \times 5 = 10$
$0 \times 0 = 0$
$30 + 16 + 50 + 10 + 0 = 106$

Answers

1

Ⓐ 18 minutes

Ⓑ 9 minutes

Ⓒ 1:23 p.m. (13:23)

2 **Math Sentence:** $3 + 2 = 5$, $5 \times 9 = 45$
Answer: 45 (blossoms)

3 **Math Sentence:** $2 \times 5 = 10$ (dollars)
　　　　　　　10 dollars − 50 cents = 9 dollars 50 cents
Answer: 9 dollars 50 cents

How to Think and Solve

1 In this problem episode, you will solve bus schedule problems. This is an application problem for time and elapsed time. If you start seeing and using mathematics in daily situations, then you will become more interested in mathematics and enjoy it more.

Ⓐ The next bus will leave at 11:05 a.m.

Ⓑ The next bus will leave at 12:35 p.m.

Ⓒ Find the time that is 48 minutes later than 12:35 p.m. There is 25 minutes between 12:35 p.m. and 1:00 p.m.
　　$48 - 25 = 23$
So, the time will be 1:23 p.m.

2 There are the same number of pink and white blossoms in each row.
You could find the total number of pink blossoms and the total number of white blossoms separately. Then, add the separate totals together to find the combined total of blossoms.

$(3 \times 9) + (2 \times 9) = 27 + 18 = 45$

You may also write the math sentence separately as shown below:

$3 \times 9 = 27,\ 2 \times 9 = 18,\ 27 + 18 = 45$

You could also solve this problem by adding the number of blossoms in one vertical column, then multiply that number by the number in each row, 9.

$(3 + 2) \times 9 = 5 \times 9 = 45$

The distributive property of multiplication is used for this second method:

$(3 \times 9) + (2 \times 9) = (3 + 2) \times 9.$

3 You need to read the conditions of the problem and determine what information is necessary and what is unnecessary to solve the problem. Jada bought 5 cans of juice, so you need to understand that the discount will be 50 cents. The problem involves dollars and cents, so please be careful converting money between dollars and cents. (Make sure you calculate dollars with dollars, and cents with cents. Don't add a number of cents to a number of dollars. They are two different units.)

Answers

1 1 hour 52 minutes

2

A **Math Sentence:** $12,040 \times 10 = 120,400$
 Answer: One hundred twenty thousand, four hundred (cookies)

B **Math Sentence:** $12,040 \times 100 = 1,204,000$
 Answer: One million, two hundred four thousand (candies)

C **Math Sentence:** $120,400 - 12,040 = 108,360$
 Answer: One hundred eight thousand, three hundred sixty (cookies)

How to Think and Solve

1 It is 24 minutes from 9:36 a.m. to 10:00 a.m. It is 1 hour 28 minutes from 10:00 a.m. to 11:28 a.m. The sum of 24 minutes and 1 hour 28 minutes is 1 hour 52 minutes.

\<Alternative solution\>

It takes 2 hours from 9:36 a.m. to 11:36 a.m., and 11:28 a.m. is 8 minutes earlier than 11:36 a.m. So, the answer is 1 hour 52 minutes.

2 3rd grade students usually learn large numbers up to 1,000. The larger number names and structures of "million," "billion" and "trillion" will be learned in 4th and 5th grades.

Let's think about multiplying by 10 and 100 using smaller numbers.
For example, $23 \times 10 = 230$: When a number is multiplied by 10, the number in the tens and ones place shifts to the hundreds and tens place (shifts one place to the left). The ones place becomes a zero, because the number was multiplied by 10.

For example, $23 \times 100 = 2{,}300$: When a number is multiplied by 100, the number in the tens and ones place shifts to the thousands and hundreds place (shifts two places to the left). The tens and ones places become zeros, because the number was multiplied by 100.

Now, let's apply the same process to problem **A** and **B**.

A $12{,}040 \times 10 = 120{,}400$ and **B** $12{,}040 \times 100 = 1{,}204{,}000$

It is very helpful to place a comma every three zeros (counting left from the ones place) since a new place value unit is introduced every three zeros. You can see for yourself, by comparing a thousand (1,000) to a million (1,000,000) to a trillion (1,000,000,000) and so on. When you see a zero (0) in a place value, that means there is no value in that place. So when you read a number with a 0, you do not need to read the place value. For example 2,045 is read as "two thousand, forty-five." As you can see, you don't say "hundred," because 0 is in the hundreds place.

C When you use the vertical algorithm to calculate large numbers, you calculate in the same way that you learned the calculations for numbers up to 1,000 in the 3rd grade.

$$\begin{array}{r} 1\,2\,0\,4\,0\,0 \\ -\quad 1\,2\,0\,4\,0 \\ \hline 1\,0\,8\,3\,6\,0 \end{array}$$

Answers

1

A **Math Sentence:** 2 L 400 mL + 5 L 500 mL = 7 L 900 mL

Answer: 7 L 900 mL (7,900 mL)

B **Math Sentence:** 5 L 500 mL – 2 L 400 mL = 3 L 100 mL

Answer: Bovinea produced 3 L 100 mL (3,100 mL) more milk than Buttercup.

1

A **Math Sentence:** 4 L 700 mL – 1 L 900 mL = 2 L 800 mL

Answer: 2 L 800mL (2,800 mL)

B **Math Sentence:** 3 L 600m L + 2 L 800 mL = 6 L 400 mL

Answer: 6 L 400 mL (6,400 mL)

C **Math Sentence:** 7 L – 6 L 400 mL = 600 mL

Answer: 600 mL

How to Think and Solve

The topic of this problem episode is measuring liquid volume. You will learn how to do calculations involving the liquid volume units of liter (L) and milliliter (mL). Problem **1** involves calculations that don't require you to regroup between two units. Problem **2** involves calculations with regrouping between two units.

We add and subtract liquid volumes in a similar way to how you learned to calculate length, so it is good to recall and review what you learned about calculating units of length (m, cm, mm). There are many other liquid volume units than liter and milliliter. If you are interested in knowing more about liquid volume, then you might want to spend some time learning more. For example, you may learn about deciliter (dL) and cubic centimeter (cm³ or cc) units in the metric system and fluid ounce (fl oz), cup (cp), pint (pt), quart (qt), and gallon (gal) units in the US customary system. Enjoy studying the relationship among these various liquid volume units. It is also a good idea to investigate liquid units that we use and see every day in our daily lives. Enjoy finding the answers to questions, such as:

- How much water, juice, or milk do you drink in a day?
- How much sugar or spice is in the container that your family buys at the grocery store?
- How much water can different aquariums hold?

Answers

1

Ⓐ **Math Sentence:** 3 L 700 mL + 1 L 800 mL = 5 L 500 mL

Answer: 5 L 500 mL (5,500 mL)

Ⓑ **Math Sentence:** 5 L 300 mL – 2 L 400 mL = 2 L 900 mL

Answer: 2 L 900 mL (2,900 mL)

Ⓒ **Math Sentence:** 4 L – 2 L 600 mL = 1 L 400 mL

Answer: 1 L 400 mL (1,400 mL)

Ⓓ **Math Sentence:** 1 L 8 dL + 5 dL + 2 L 9 dL = 5 L 2 dL

Answer: 5 L 2 dL (52 dL, 5200 mL)

Ⓔ **Answer:** Monday

This problem episode includes calculations of liter (L), milliliter (mL), and deciliter (dL) units. The deciliter unit is not commonly used in the US, but it is challenging to think about the relationship among different units in problem-solving situations on your own.

1 For problems **A** and **B**, you are asked to solve calculation problems involving liter and milliliter units including regrouping between these units. Previously, you have done similar calculations with units of length, so you may want to think about what you learned when calculating lengths.

C The minuend doesn't include the milliliter unit. Because you need to regroup between units, it is a good idea to split 4 L into 3 L and 1,000 mL.

D This problem involves a new unfamiliar liquid unit, the deciliter (dL). It also includes three addends. The addition of digits in deciliter units is 8 dL + 5 dL + 9 dL = 22 dL. 1 liter is equal to 10 deciliters, so 22 dL is equal to 2 L 2 dL.

E When comparing liquid quantities, it is a good idea to make sure all quantities are expressed in the same unit. So, convert 5 L 2 dL into 5 L 200 mL to compare with other quantities that include milliliters (mL).

Answers

1

A Left side plate --- (C), Right side plate --- (A)

B 2 g, 6 g, 10 g

C 1 g, 3 g, 9 g

2 B

How to Think and Solve

1 In Problem Episode No.40 and No.41, you will solve balance scale application problems.

A You need to think about making the weight on the left side 7 g heavier than the weight on the right side. When you put the 8 g weight on the left side and the 1 g weight on the right side, the left side is 7 g heavier (8 − 1 = 7).
When you put the 8 g weight on the left side and the 1 g weight and 7 g salt on the right side, you can represent this in a math sentence:
8 g = 1 g + 7 g
The equal sign (=) means that values on each side of the equal sign are the same. In other words, both sides are balanced. The math sentence is like a balance scale!

B 1, 3 = 4 − 1, 4, 5 = 1 + 4,
7 = 8 − 1, 8, 9 = 1 + 8,
11 = 4 + 8 − 1, 12 = 4 + 8
13 = 1 + 4 + 8

C This is a very difficult problem. This problem helps you to develop logical thinking and perseverance. Don't give up easily. Think about the problem for a couple of days and don't feel bad about that. In math, it is often necessary to take time and persevere (keep at it!). Many great mathematicians think about a problem for days and sometimes years!
You need to think about other combinations of

three weights that make 13 g. For example:
1 g, 3 g, and 9 g; 1 g, 2 g, and 10 g; 2 g, 3 g, and 8 g; etc.

Then you need to think about whether or not you can measure all the weights from 1 g through 13 g and still use the balance scale only one time.

If you use 1 g, 3 g, and 9 g weights, you can measure all the weights as shown here:

$1, \ 2 = 3 - 1, \ 3, \ 1 + 3 = 4,$
$5 = 9 - 1 - 3, \ 6 = 9 - 3,$
$7 = 1 + 9 - 3, \ 8 = 9 - 1,$
$9, \ 10 = 1 + 9, \ 11 = 3 + 9 - 1$
$12 = 3 + 9, \ 13 = 1 + 3 + 9$

2 There are several ways to solve this problem. Below are two different ways to solve the puzzle.

Solution Example 1:
- From the picture in the middle, you can see that coins A and C are the same weight. So, one of the B, D, and E coins has a different weight.
- From the picture on the left, you can tell that one of the coins B or D has a different weight, because coins A and C are the same weight. Since the scale is not balanced and coin E is not on the scale, coin E must be the same weight as coins A and C.
- From the picture on the right, you can tell that coin B is the coin with a different weight (B is heavier than the other coins), because coins A, C, and E are the same weight.

Solution Example 2:
- From the picture on the left, you can tell that coin E is not the coin with a different weight, because the scale is not balanced.

- From the picture in the middle, you can see that coins A and C are the same weight. So, neither can be the coin that has a different weight, because there is only one coin with a different weight.
- From the picture on the left, you can tell that coin D must weigh the same as A, C, and E, because the scale is not balanced. From this observation, you can conclude that coins A, C, D, and E are the same weight.

Answers

1 The first time: 3 coins

The second time: 1 coin

2 3 times

How to Think and Solve

1 When Ms. Rice said putting 1 coin each on both sides of the scale will probably take many trials (times) to figure out the problem, you may have thought about putting 4 coins each on both sides of the scale. In this case, if the scale balances, the one you did not put on the scale is the heavy one. (This way you can find the heavy coin the first time!) If the scale does not balance, the lower plate contains the heavier coin. However, it will not be possible to find the heavy coin the second time. If you put 2 coins each on both sides of the scale, one of the sides will be lower but you are not able to identify which one of the two coins on the heavier side is really the heavier coin. So you would need to use the scale one more time.

Logically, you may think about putting 3 coins on both sides of the scale.

1. If the scale balances, the heavy coin is one of the 3 coins you did not put on the scale. For the second time, use the 3 coins you did not use the first time. Put 1 coin each on both sides. If the scale balances, the coin you did not put on the scale is the heavy one. If the scale does not balance, the heavier (lower) side holds the heavy coin.

2. When you put 3 coins each on both sides of the scale and the scale does not balance, you need to investigate the 3 coins on the heavy side a second time. Put 1 of these coins on each side of the scale. If the scale balances, the one you did not put on the scale is the

heavy one. If the scale does not balance, the heavier (lower) side holds the heavy coin.

The answer involves putting 3 coins each on both sides the first time and 1 coin each on both sides the second time.

2 This is a difficult problem because you can use a weight of salt as a new weight the next time you use the scale. In addition, you need to think about what amount of salt you want to measure each time, so you can be sure the total salt measured is 40 g. You may want to draw diagrams or create tables to organize your thinking and keep track of the weights and the results of your efforts.

You can use the scale to weigh 40 g of salt in the least number of times as described below.

1. Put a 1 g weight and a 6 g weight on the left-side plate. Then, put salt on the right-side plate until the scale balances. When you put 7 g of salt on the scale it will balance.
   $1 g + 6 g = 7 g$

2. Put the 6 g weight on the right-side plate with the 7 g salt you measured the first time. Then, put salt on the left side until the scale balances. When you put 13 g of salt on the left side, the scale will balance. $13 g = 7 g + 6 g$

3. Put the 7 g and 13 g of salt that you measured on the left-side plate. Then, put salt on the right-side plate until the scale balances. When you put 20 g of salt on the scale, it will balance. $7 g + 13 g = 20 g$

   Now you have 7 g, 13 g and 20 g of salt on the scale. If you add them all, the total weight of salt will be $7 g + 13 g + 20 g = 40 g$.

You can measure 40 g of salt using the scale 3 times.

Answers

1 D

2

Ⓐ [Example]

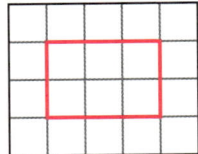

Ⓑ [Example]

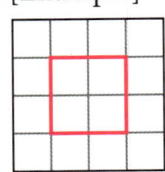

Ⓒ [Example]

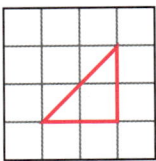

3
Ⓐ C, E, F (you may record answers in any order)
Ⓑ E
Ⓒ G

How to Think and Solve

1 This problem checks if you can identity right angles intuitively (without exact measurements).

2 The length of each side of a square in the grid is 1 cm, so you can use this measurement to draw the shapes. When you draw lines in mathematics, you are often asked to use a straightedge (or ruler) to draw the lines accurately. It is a good idea to use a straightedge often, so you get used to drawing lines and geometric figures very precisely.

3 This problem asks you to identify quadrilaterals, squares, and right triangles.

Ⓐ Quadrilaterals are closed figures with four straight lines. Shape A is not a quadrilateral because it has a curved line.

Ⓑ Please check that shape E has four sides of equal length.

Answers

1

A 4

B **Math Sentence:** [Example] $4 \times 4 = 16$

Answer: 16

2 **Math Sentence:** [Example] $7 \times 3 = 21$

Answer: 21

3 **Math Sentence:** [Example]

$$4 + 2 = 6 \qquad 4 + 6 = 10$$
$$10 \times 2 = 20$$

Answer: 20

4 **Math Sentence:** [Example]

$$3 \text{ cm } 5 \text{ mm} + 2 \text{ cm } 5 \text{ mm} = 6 \text{ cm}$$
$$6 \times 2 = 12$$

Answer: 12

How to Think and Solve

1 Math sentence "4 + 4 + 4 + 4" is also correct and will lead to the correct answer. However, it is better to write a multiplication sentence, 4×4, to demonstrate that you know how to represent multiples in a multiplication sentence.

2 Math sentence "7 + 7 + 7" is also correct, but it is better to represent the relationship in a written multiplication sentence, 7×3 (or 3×7).

3 Find the length of the longer side first. Use the property of rectangles: the facing two sides are equal in length. Add the lengths of a short side and a long side, then multiply that sum by 2 to find the perimeter. The perimeter (complete length around the rectangle) is $(4 + 6) \times 2$. Other math sentences that are also correct are "4 + 6 + 4 + 6" or "$4 \times 2 + 6 \times 2$."

4 The math sentence "3 cm 5 mm + 2 cm 5 mm + 3 cm 5 mm + 2 cm 5 mm" is correct, because math sentences generally use the numbers as written in a problem. However, the math sentence "35 mm + 25 mm + 35 mm + 25 mm" which uses all measurements in the same unit, millimeters, is also acceptable and correct.

Answers

1

Ⓐ 132 cm²   Ⓑ 92 m²

Ⓒ 540 m²

2

Ⓐ 350,000 cm²   Ⓑ 144 ft²

3 375 cm²

How to Think and Solve

1

Ⓐ You can find the area by subtracting the area of the square from the large rectangle. Look at diagram 1 below. The length of the unknown side of the large rectangle can be found by 3 + 6 + 5 = 14 (cm).

So, the area can be found by 14 × 12 − 6 × 6 = 132 (cm²)

Also, you may solve this by dividing the shape into three parts horizontally as shown in diagram 2.

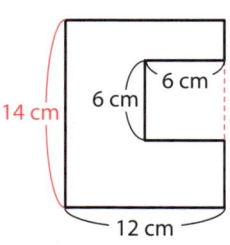 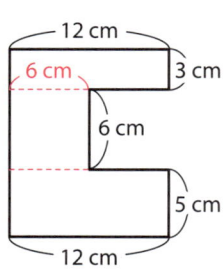

Diagram 1   Diagram 2

Ⓑ Think about subtracting the area of the square inside the area of the rectangle.

12 × 9 − 4 × 4 = 92 (m²)

Ⓒ Look at diagram 3 below. You can think about subtracting a small rectangle and a square from the area of the large rectangle,

12 + 22 = 34 (The length of the large rectangle)

10 + 14 = 24 (The width of the large rectangle)

24 − 16 = 8 (The width of the small rectangle to be subtracted)

So, 34 × 24 − 22 × 8 − 10 × 10 = 540 (m²)

Please add 14 m in diagram 3 just like the original figure.

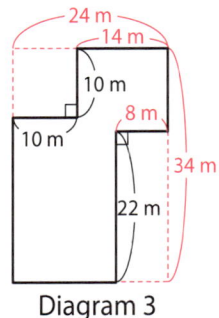

Diagram 3

2

Ⓐ The rectangle has a 5 m length and a 7 m width. First, think about how many cm the length and width are: 5 m = 500 cm and 7 m = 700 cm

So, the area of the rectangle in cm² can be found by 500 × 700 = 350,000 (cm²)

Ⓑ The side of the square is 4 yards. So, 4 yards is 4 × 3 = 12 (ft). (1 yd = 3 ft) So, the area of the square in ft² can be found by 12 × 12 = 144 (ft²) It is a good idea for you to investigate the relationship of area units in the metric system and the US customary system.

3 Look at the diagram below. If you combine area A and area C, $(20 \times 2 - 5) \times 5 = 175$ (cm²).
That is the same as combining area B and area D.
Then, area E is $5 \times 5 = 25$ (cm²).
So, the area that is asked for in this problem is $175 \times 2 + 25 = 375$ (cm²).

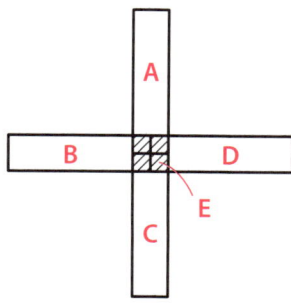

You can solve it in the following way as well.
The total area of four tapes is:
$5 \times 20 \times 4 = 400$ (cm²).
But there are overlapping areas.

The overlapping part E has two layers.
So, if you subtract the overlapping areas once from the total area of four tapes, you will find the area of the shape.
$400 - 5 \times 5 = 375$ (cm²)

Answers

1

Ⓐ 780 m² 　　　　Ⓑ 130 m²

Ⓒ 10 m

2

Ⓐ 4,956 m² 　　　　Ⓑ 4,602 m²

How to Think and Solve

1 Area B is five times as much as area A. So, the whole area (the sum of areas A and B) is $1 + 5 = 6$ times as much as area A.
If you divide area B into five equal parts as shown in the diagram below, it is easy to under-stand this.

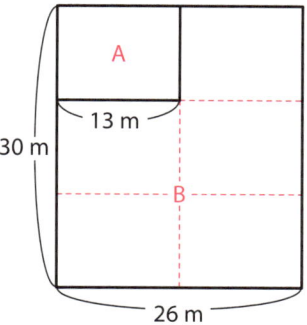

2 The area of paths doesn't change when you move the position of the paths. So, the shaded area is equal to the rectangles as shown below.

Ⓐ
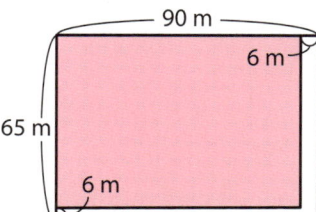

Ⓑ
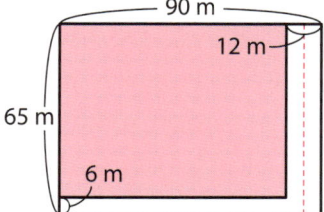

149

Z-kai Zoom-Up Workbook Math   Grade 3

◼ Authors

Advisory and Editorial Board: Makoto Yoshida, Ph.D.

Dr. Makoto Yoshida is the Director of Curriculum and Professional Development at East West Math LLC, a mathematics education consulting company he co-founded. His service to schools and teachers is comprehensive and presently includes international consulting and professional development for lower-secondary mathematics teachers in Thailand, through the Consortium for Policy Research in Education (CPRE), Teachers College, Columbia University. He served as the president of Association of Mathematics Teachers of New Jersey (AMTNJ) in 2017. Through his work, his interests include helping teachers improve their content knowledge, problem-solving pedagogy, lesson study and instructional use of tools and models, all in the service of fostering students' deeper understanding and avid interest in learning mathematics. Dr. Yoshida earned his Ph.D. from the University of Chicago.

Editorial Staff: Mary N. Leer, Ed.D.

Dr. Mary N. Leer is the director of the educational consulting firm Visualizing Education, Reframing Achievement (VERA): Leer Educational Consulting LLC, and a supervised fieldwork advisor for the Leadership in Mathematics Education program of the Bank Street Graduate School of Education, NYC. Her consulting interests include: editing and writing curricular materials with a special focus on making Singapore and Japanese curricular materials and pedagogy accessible to U.S. teachers; providing professional development for teachers focused on the development of number sense, strategic fluency, and problem-solving pedagogy. The passion that drives her interests is the desire to see the success and joy of learning math come alive for all students. She earned her Ed.D. from Widener University.

◼ Z-kai Learning Materials Development Division

First published on April 10, 2020

Visit Zoom-Up Workbook website at https://zkaibooks.com

Published by Z-kai Inc.

1-9-11, Bunkyo-cho, Mishima-shi, Shizuoka, Japan

E-mail: books-us@zkai.co.jp

Website: https://service.zkai.co.jp/home/corporate/english/index.html

---

© Z-kai Inc. 2020

All rights reserved.

No part of this book may be reproduced, stored in a retrieval system or transmitted in any form or by any means, electronic, mechanical, photocopying, recording or otherwise, without permission of the Publisher.
Printed in Japan.

ISBN 978-4-86290-3198

Z-KAI